# ARCHITECTURE IN THE SEVENTIES

# ARCHITECTURE IN THE SEVENTIES

Udo Kultermann

**Architectural Book Publishing Company**
**New York 10016**

*Frontispiece: Montgomerie, Oldfield and Kirby's staff
maisonettes for the Bank of Zambia (see page 113)*

© Udo Kultermann 1980

First published in 1980 by The Architectural Press Ltd: London

Published 1980 in the U.S.A.
by Architectural Book Publishing Co. Inc.

Library of Congress Cataloging In Publication Data

Kultermann, Udo.
  Architecture in the seventies.
  1. Architecture, Modern—20th century.
  2. Vernacular architecture.    3. Architecture—Human
factors.    I. Title.
  NA680.K788 1980    724.9'1    80-19744

  ISBN 0-8038-0019-3

Printed in Great Britain by BAS Printers Limited
Over Wallop, Hampshire

# Contents

# Introduction

## INTRODUCTION
### From the Sixties to the Seventies

Periods of artistic endeavour, like periods of history, can be broadly characterised as being turbulent or stable. Certainly the seventies fall into the former category and this circumstance makes the task of selecting buildings to represent it an inevitably controversial one. In the sixties one could still have some sort of consensus about a characteristic style, influenced as this and earlier decades were by the surviving masters of the Modern Movement. In the seventies there were still buildings that reflected and harked back to this heroic and hopeful age, but the echoes were becoming increasingly faint and interrupted by noises off-stage. There was, throughout the world, a loss of confidence in what had been regarded as established architectural values; these were challenged by the social failure of prestigious housing projects, by the energy crisis, by the fact that voices proclaiming that at least some architectural emperors were dressed in new clothes were becoming increasingly audible, by the return to vernacular styles and methods which was engendered by the belief that the past offered answers to the questions of the present in both social and technological terms.

Some architects, of course, went on designing sixties' buildings in the seventies and no doubt the illustrations in this book will spark off a good deal of argument about what is and is not a characteristic building of its period. What is certain is that the reaction of architects to the challenge of the seventies was not dependent on the age of the designer. The generation whose work is represented in this book ranges from Ralph Erskine (b. 1914) and Harry Weese (b. 1915) to those who were actually born after the Second World War. Being responsive to what was going on in the seventies was then a matter of attitude rather than age; which is not to decry the pioneering work that emerged in the sixties. It was William Morris who said that the Arts and Crafts Movement would not have been possible without Pugin and in the same way one can say that without the liberating influence of the sixties—and even including that decade's descent into 'swinging sixties' silliness and excess—the most exciting and innovatory aspects of seventies' architecture would not have been possible.

One such aspect was the revival of interest in decoration that began to emerge in the sixties' work of such architects as Kenzo Tange, Paul Rudolph and Roche and Dinkeloo. Though they saw themselves as irreproachable heirs of the masters of the Modern Movement, with whom they had in fact stood in direct contact, the way they used new materials and deployed structural forms was a departure from the ideas of such men as Gropius, Mies van der Rohe and Le Corbusier. The one master who did turn out to have a dominating influence, though, was Louis Kahn, who had previously been a somewhat isolated figure, out of the mainstream of the Modern Movement. It was his attitude to form, his advocacy of humanistic values and his insistence on the irrational and the emotional in architecture that provided a rationale for what was to follow. His presence can be sensed behind the work of people like Charles Moore and Robert Venturi who re-examined the nature of vernacular in an industrial world; of Aldo van Eyck and Giancarlo de Carlo who turned their backs on theoretical abstractions in getting to grips with constructional reality; and of Aldo Rossi, James Stirling and Richard Meier, all of whom struck out along individualistic paths of form and content that were increasingly remote from the unobtrusive and eventually anonymous functionalism of the Modern Movement's severer purists.

One consequence of the return in the sixties to a pre-

1

occupation with form which we would now feel to have been less than happy was the way public buildings were sometimes articulated as romantic bastions of power and influence to echo the shape of military architecture and other kinds of fortifications. However, there was also and at the same time a counter-cultural movement towards self-help buildings, geodesic domes and various earnest, if confused attempts to arrive at an architecture without buildings, sparked off by the instant tent cities of rock festivals which themselves probably emanated from a sympathy, fashionable among the young, for a nomadic life style, uncluttered by either social obligations or physical possessions.

Though none of these trends survived as such into the seventies, they can still be perceived in a transmuted form. Individualism, decoration and the plastic manipulation of the built form did not disappear, but became subordinated to a much greater degree of social involvement by designers; or, to put it more simply, a greater awareness of who buildings were going to be used by, and for what purpose. John Andrew's Cameron offices in Canberra (p. 129) and Harry Weese's Oak Park City Hall (p. 17) were indeed commissioned by public authorities, but with their humanistic preoccupations, they are fundamentally different from government buildings of the sixties, such as Boston's imposing City Hall, or those monumental government centres of a previous decade Chandigarh and Brasilia; and this is even more true of buildings with a specific social purpose such as Richard Meier's Bronx Development Center (p. 4) and Stanley Tigerman's Library for the Blind in Chicago (p. 14).

Even office buildings, whose façades at any rate had been a direct expression of the power and achievement of the client company—typified by works like Mies van der Rohe's Seagram Building or Roche and Dinkeloo's Ford Foundation—began to reflect in the seventies a much more equivocal attitude towards corporate power. The best-known example of this has been Herman Hertzberger's Central Beheer at Apeldorn (p. 35) with its wide open interior spaces, designed not only to accommodate business but to give every employee a sense of personal space. It is true that the interiors of some sixties' office buildings paid more attention to individual needs than their exteriors suggested, but it is not until the seventies that in offices like the Central Beheer exteriors and interiors are in complete harmony, the one articulating the other and thus giving expression to Hertzberger's affirmation: 'What we must look for, in the place of prototypes which are collective interpretations of individual living patterns, are prototypes which make individual interpretations of the collective patterns possible'.

The same seventies' theme—the emphasis on the importance of individual needs over corporate images—can also be seen in some of the other building types illustrated in this volume. For example, universities shown here are either workers' universities like the Spanish Technical University of Almeria by Cano Lasso and Campo Baeza (p. 76) or the new kind of university, like Virta's Oulu University in Finland, which is based on the concept of participation in and integration with the community rather than being an elitist temple of learning.

A similar notion pervades the typical seventies' museum in Moenchengladbach by Hans Hollein (p. 47) which is intended to be part of the urban infrastructure rather than a separate cultural sanctum. The same could be said of Sumet Jumsai's non-monumental science museum in Bangkok, designed to invite the average citizen to participate in the wonders of science; or of Piano and Rogers' Centre Pompidou in Paris (p. 52), with its aim of making culture part of the business of everyday living. On the other hand, illustrating the fact that architectural eras cannot be neatly compartmentalised, Tao Ho's Hong Kong Arts Centre is a typical sixties' building even though completed in 1977.

It may well be, however, that the museum of the past is itself a thing of the past. The trend now—again arising from a heightened social awareness—is for them to be integrated into an overall leisure and recreational context, designed to enrich the quality of life. An example of this type of complex is the Hall in Mannheim by Carlfried Mutschler and Frei Otto (p. 38), as is the Aquarium in Okinawa by Fumihiko Maki (p. 146). In the USSR, the Leisure building in Voronovo by I Cherniavskii, I Popov and I Vasilevski (p. 93) is part of a government programme to 'enhance the physical well-being of its citizens'.

Where the theme that emerged strongly from the architecture of the sixties—the search for a new and socially more sensitive way of expressing built forms—found its most frequent manifestation was in a building type we have so far not mentioned: housing. In many ways everything else that has happened in architecture in the sixties and seventies is unimportant compared to the battle for the soul of architecture which began when it became clear that the heroic gestures of the sixties, like Moshe Safdie's Habitat, simply did not work in human, economic or even technical terms. Some of the most significant buildings of the seventies direct themselves to this problem; successfully in the case of Moshe Safdie's Coldspring New Town in Baltimore (p. 11), a scheme which, though not as spectacular as Habitat, did actually achieve some of the more famous Montreal building's aims; successfully also, it appears, in Ralph Erskine's Byker Redevelopment at Newcastle-upon-Tyne (p. 31), a fascinating and widely discussed attempt to make user participation in the design process more than mere lip service; and rather less successfully in a similar venture by Giancarlo de Carlo in Terni (p. 65) where the personal wishes of the residents eventually became too demanding to be practicable. Charles Moore emphasised the importance of housing in architectural thinking by saying, 'we have become very interested in the urgencies of larger housing groups where the need has been not only to make the center of the world for an individual family, but to figure out how at minimum cost and with some density, to put these centers of the world together without losing their uniqueness'. It follows then that many of the schemes shown in this book, ranging from Runcorn to Jerusalem and from Finland to India, are concerned with public housing; undoubtedly the dominant preoccupation of seventies' architecture.

If one can no longer talk about architecture without a fundamental re-interpretation of social issues, equally it is no longer possible to divorce it from a new, revisionist view of political and economic forces. The uncritical acceptance of the International Style in developing countries which marked the period up to the end of the sixties has been replaced by a much greater appreciation of local cultural needs and traditions as well as of the appropriateness of indigenous technology. Some of this 'vernacular' building has expressed itself in specious idioms, more related to Disneyland than to the real world. But as countries become more sophisticated, so, hopefully, does the grasp of their own traditions become firmer. This is particularly noticeable in Japan in works by local architects such as Isozaki, Maki (p. 146) and Kurokawa (p. 136); in Latin American buildings by Perez de Arce and Clorindo Testa; in Africa in Faraoui and de Mazières' hotel in Morocco (p. 109), in buildings by Hassan Fathy in Egypt and by Oluwole Olumuyiwa in Lagos, Nigeria; and in Australia where John Andrews expresses a certain Australian identity in his designs. Even where countries have brought in architects from abroad, they have attempted to adapt to the local tradition rather than bringing an international style with them, as can be seen in Lima, Peru in the work there of such people as Tovio Korhonen (p. 105), Stirling and van Eyck from Europe, Correa from India and Kikutake and Kurokawa from Japan.

But it is not only in developing countries that there has been a return to the past in a search for design solutions appropriate to the future. In other countries there has also been a realisation that without historical awareness, scholarship even, the goals of producing a viable architecture for the seventies cannot be met in either aesthetic or technical terms. For it is not only that the architecture of the past seemed to do its job more successfully both socially and visually; it also offers insights into the solution of what many people think will be the major problem of the remainder of this century; namely the gathering energy crisis. Yet the architecture of the seventies has not turned its back on the future; rather, it has become respectful of the past and the tension between these two themes make the buildings in this book so fascinating to study.

*View of the pedestrian zone in Gottfried Böhm's housing scheme at Chorweiler, Cologne, West Germany, which was completed in 1974*

USA

## RICHARD MEIER
### Bronx Developmental Center,
### the Bronx, New York
### (1970—76)

The Borough Developmental Services Office is a new organisation which coordinates state, city, and voluntary agencies to create a system of services for disabled and mentally retarded people who live in the Bronx. One of its new facilities is the Bronx Developmental Center at 1200 Waters Place. In its function, design and choice of building material, this center stands as an outstanding example of architecture in the seventies.

It was originally conceived to house 750 physically disabled and mentally retarded children, but eventually it was redesigned to service out-patients, with 380 places for resident patients.

The complex is divided into two wings. One is for out-patients and administration, the other is residential. They are built around a large inner garden, and connected by a section which contains a therapeutic pool and large gymnasium. The total complex is oriented inwards. In isolating itself from the outside environment, it presents the only possible solution to the problem of its industrial location. The building material is aluminium which creates a smooth, shiny surface.

In creating this centre the architect has made a statement in built form which is practical, durable, and creates a sense of identity in the patients. It is this sense of place and identity which becomes the central focus of this architectural masterpiece.

*The centre seen from the park (above)*

*Staircase leading to connecting corridor (above, top)*

*The centre seen from the street side (left)*

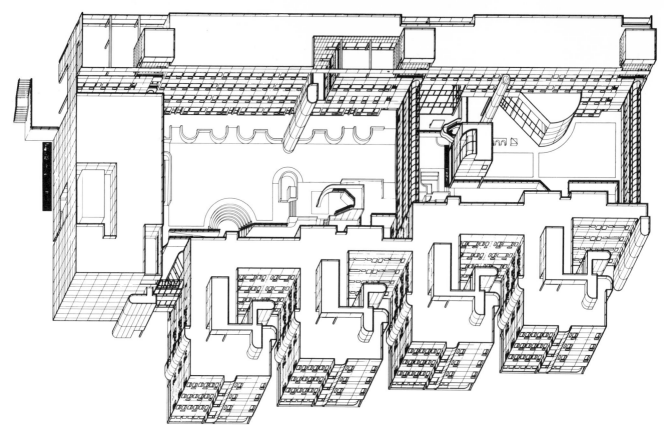

*Axonometric scheme*

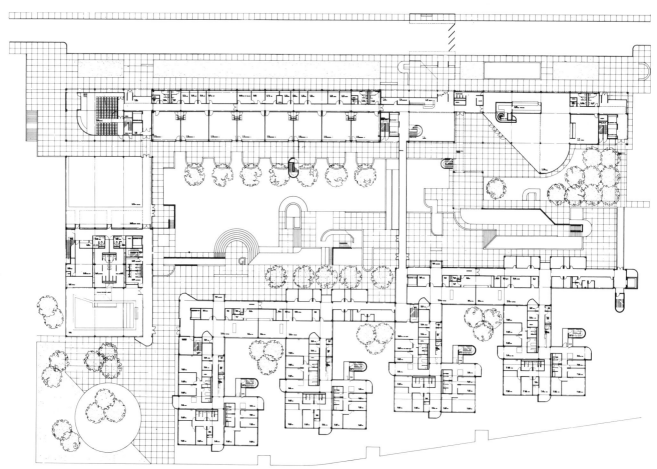

*Ground floor plan*

*Detail of experimental unit in the courtyard (opposite)*

# MOORE GROVER HARPER
## Whitman Village Housing, Huntington, Long Island, New York
### (1971–75)

The Whitman Village Housing was part of an urban renewal plan in the town of Huntington in 1968. The goal of the architect was to establish a small neighbourhood with its own identity. The village includes 21 four-family houses, 88 town houses with two, four, and five bedrooms and 88 one-bedroom apartments, totalling 260 units. They are inhabited by low and moderate income families; the density is 18·47 units per acre. Near by is a community building, and there are future plans for a commercial area.

The houses are arranged in a way that protects the garden areas in between, which is in harmony with the tradition of housing on Long Island. The structures are wooden frame with shingles as the skin material.

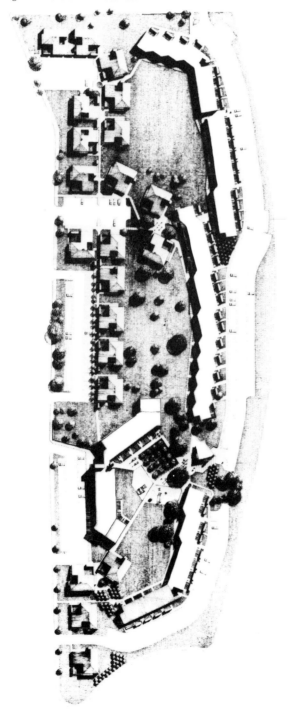

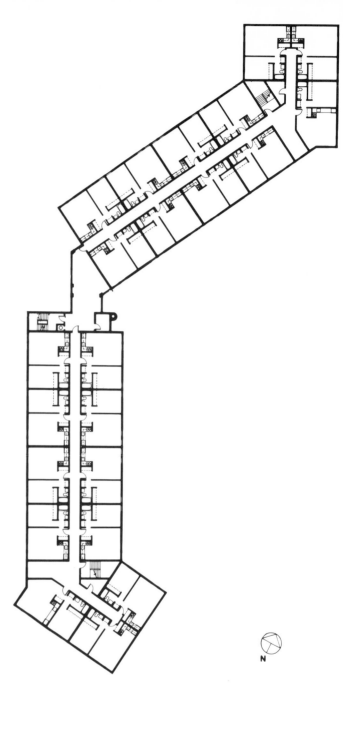

*Site plan of the village*

*Typical floor plan of an apartment block*

*Two views of a row of four-family houses (opposite)*

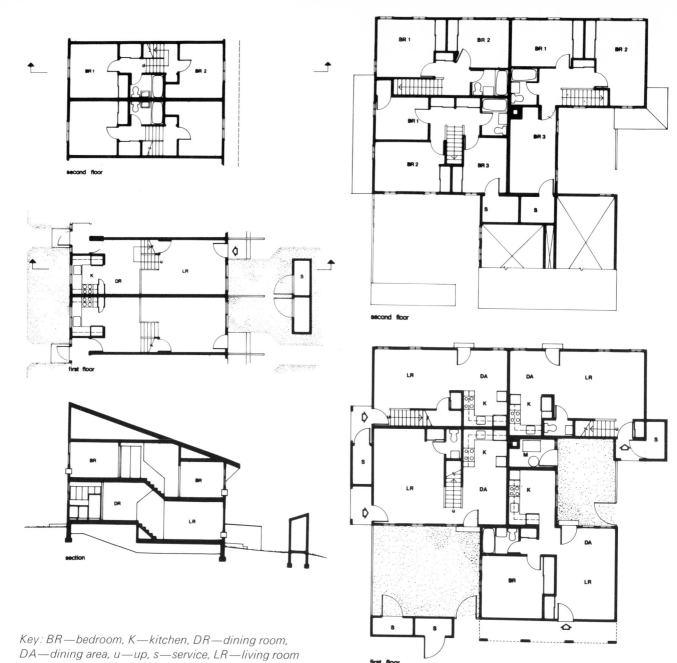

second floor

first floor

section

Key: BR—bedroom, K—kitchen, DR—dining room,
DA—dining area, u—up, s—service, LR—living room

*Sections and plans of a town house*

second floor

first floor

*Floor plans of a four-family house*

# MOSHE SAFDIE
## Coldspring New Town, Baltimore, Maryland (1970–78)

Coldspring New Town is a newly built suburb of the city of Baltimore. Planning began in 1968 for 370 acres of predominantly vacant hillside in Baltimore, designed to follow the example of mid-town housing built in Montreal in 1967. The total number of units planned is 3,780, of which 70% are condominiums and 30% rented accomodation, with an estimated population of 12,500 people. The cost of the individual houses ranges from $33,000 to $60,000.

The type of housing differs throughout the suburb. Town houses in groups of 15 to 30 are built along the sides of a pedestrian deck which covers the common parking area. Construction of the houses is by traditional means: concrete blockwork and infill walls of stucco and double glass. Different groups of town houses are connected by ramps or bridges and a complete separation of pedestrian and vehicular traffic is achieved.

A second type of housing is designed for the hillside sites and is clustered into buildings of six or seven units on four main levels. A third type of housing is apartment buildings adjacent to the local centres. One of these is a 20-storey building built in an abandoned quarry which is entered from above.

The total community is composed of three overlapping areas, with a local centre which contains an elementary school and other community facilities. A town centre is also planned with a middle school, shops, offices, and social facilities.

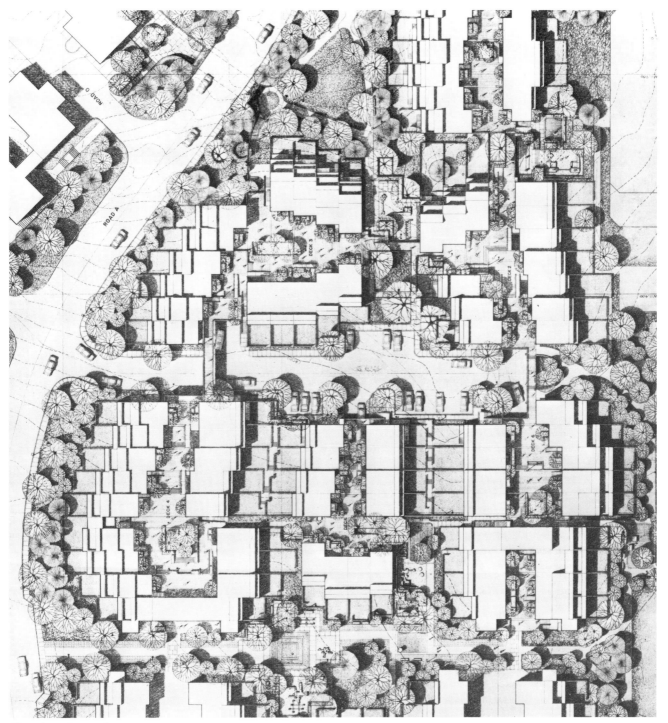

*Site plan of town houses*

Townhouses in Coldspring

Section through town houses

Master plan model: aerial view from the north (opposite)

## STANLEY TIGERMANN
### Illinois Regional Library for the Blind and Physically Handicapped and Community Library, Chicago, Illinois (1976–78)

This building, on a triangular site southwest of the Chicago Circle Campus, has three main purposes: it serves as the distribution centre for books and cassettes for the handicapped in the state of Illinois; it is the Chicago library for the blind and handicapped; it is the branch library for the inner-city community. The architect successfully defined space for specified needs.

The main feature of the interior is based on circulation, with linear elements and strong colours applied as orientation aids. The furniture is built-in, and thus is always in the same place, making it easy for the blind to find. The exterior walls are structured with strongly coloured metal panels, and the undulating horizontal window on the main wall is similar to the interior walls, which direct the blind user through the building. Everything within the building is designed in soft or round shapes in order to prevent accidents while serving as further guides for the users. On the first floor there is a branch library and offices for people who are not handicapped, as well as a playground for children.

*Main entrance (right)*

*Main wall—interior; the undulating window shape and interior walls help to guide the blind (opposite)*

*Pieces of fitted furniture also act as landmarks for the blind (below)*

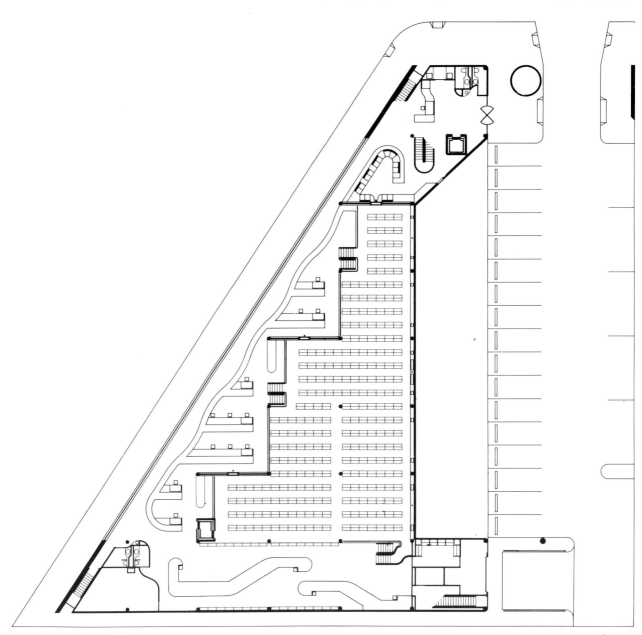

Ground floor plan

Main wall—exterior

## HARRY WEESE
## Village Hall, Oak Park, Illinois
## (1971–74)

This small administration centre is located in the environment of Frank Lloyd Wright's architecture in Oak Park. The scale of this small community was expressed in this 70,000 sq ft building which surrounds a central square courtyard open to the public. Cultural and administrative functions are separated from the commercially oriented environment, echoing the Town Hall at Saeynaetsalo in Finland by Alvar Aalto of 1950–1952. Aalto's work is one of the major architectural masterpieces articulating the relationship between government and people governed. Weese's reference to Aalto's Town Hall is intentional and gives additional meaning to the building.

At one corner of the site is a triangular building which contains the 140-seat Council Chamber. This building, which is elevated and overlooks a pool and fountain, has received particular emphasis. Either side of it is an entrance way into the inner courtyard, symbolic of the village square. As in Aalto's Town Hall, here the building material is common brick which is in the local tradition. Large round windows draw attention to the important sections of the building.

*Ramp leading to the interior court*

*Aerial view of the Village Hall*

*Entrance to the main lobby*

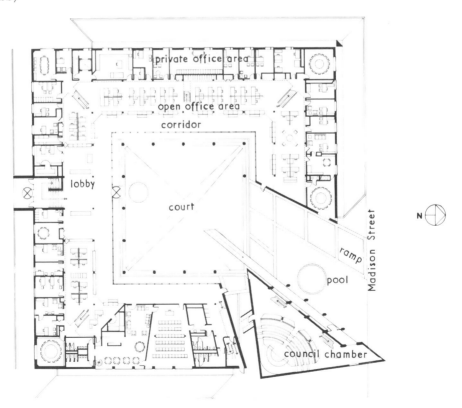

*Main level plan*

The elevated, triangular-shaped building which houses the council chamber

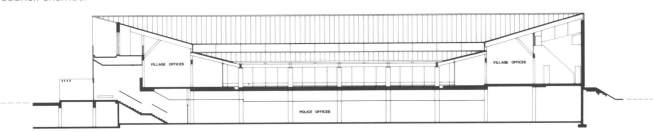

North-south section

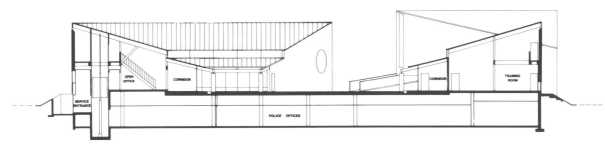

East-west section

# Canada

## RICHARD E. HULBERT AND PARTNERS
### Housing, Coquitlam, British Columbia (1975)

Housing in harmony with local climate and topography is reflected in the 58 condominiums in Coquitlam by the firm of R. E. Hulbert of Vancouver. The units, which are arranged in two building blocks, are wood-frame constructions on a site which slopes upwards from the street at the south boundary. The density is 30 units per acre. There is a golf course immediately adjacent to the site. The two blocks are each three storeys high, with garages under each building. The condominium units are either split level, two-storey town houses, or corner bungalows. Their sizes range from 1100 to 1600 sq ft. The conventional enclosed access corridors are replaced by multiple access ways. The split level units and corner bungalows are entered from the parking deck; the town houses are entered from a third floor pedestrian landscaped street with a skylight above. All condominiums have two means of access or exit for safety and convenience.

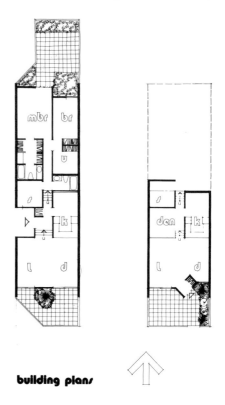

**building plans**

Key: MBR—master bedroom, BR—bedroom, K—kitchen, L—living area, D—dining area, den—study

*Split-level condominium showing alternative plans for the living area (above)*

*Pedestrian street (opposite)*

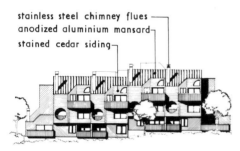

stainless steel chimney flues
anodized aluminium mansard
stained cedar siding

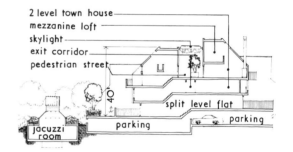

2 level town house
mezzanine loft
skylight
exit corridor
pedestrian street

40'

jacuzzi room

parking

split level flat

parking

*View (top)*

*Side elevation and section (above)*

*Site plan (right)*

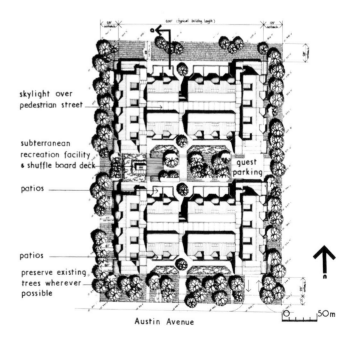

skylight over
pedestrian street

subterranean
recreation facility
& shuffle board deck

patios

guest
parking

patios

preserve existing
trees wherever
possible

Austin Avenue

0          50m

## GUSTAVO DA ROZA
## The Winnipeg Art Gallery,
## Winnipeg, Manitoba
## (1969–1971)

The shape of the art gallery in Manitoba is rather unusual. The triangular site in the centre of the city was chosen to create an image directly in the midst of public life. The building is in reinforced concrete. Its shape, in response to the challenge of the site, has become its central feature.

The ground floor contains the entrance, lobby, and a large auditorium in which the stage uses the triangular corner to the utmost. On the mezzanine floor are offices, library, drawing and print rooms, and the Art Education Department. The main gallery space is divided into nine smaller galleries, which are flexible because of their semi-permanent wall structure. On the roof of the gallery is a restaurant and coffee shop and a sculpture garden.

*Entrance*

LONGITUDINAL SECTION  0  8  16

*Section*

24

*Sculpture display on roof*

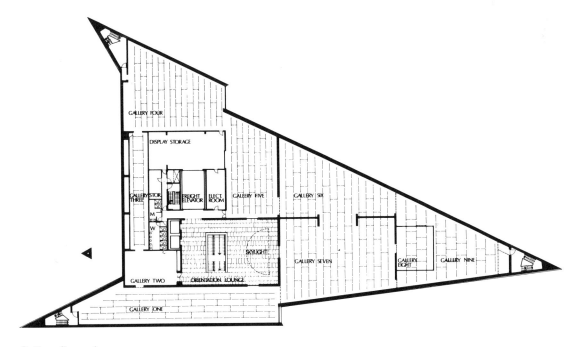

*Gallery floor plan*

*View showing roof area (left)*

25

# United Kingdom

## JAMES STIRLING
### Housing, Runcorn New Town, Cheshire (1967–76)

The goal of the client was to relieve the housing shortage in the two large neighbouring cities of Liverpool and Manchester. To house 1500 families, Stirling inaugurated, in line with older repetitive housing systems in England (Queen's Square in Bath and Bedford Place in London), a contemporary form. The basic concept is the arrangement of closed-in courts surrounded by terrace housing, creating peaceful inside garden spaces.

The access to outside traffic areas is by foot ramps and a pedestrian bridge leading directly to the town centre. The dimensions of the smallest garden square in Runcorn are 300 × 300 ft, the largest is 600 × 600 ft. There are no through streets in the whole complex. The idea of footways on the third level of the housing in Runcorn has another analogy in tradition—it recreates the rows of the nearby town of Chester.

Stirling's five-storey blocks each consist of three different size units. There is a two-storey dwelling for five or six people, with kitchen, dining and play area on the ground level, which opens to a private garden. The bedrooms are on the second level. The second two-storey dwelling, occupying the third and fourth levels, is for four or five occupants. Access is from the footpath on the third level, which the kitchen looks on to. The living room opens onto a large balcony overlooking the green square below, the bedrooms occupy the upper storey. On the fifth floor is an apartment for single people, or young married couples. It is accessible from a staircase leading up from the third level footpath, and it too has a large balcony.

The bedrooms in all the units have circular windows. All the living rooms and balconies are designed to overlook the inside square. The garages and parking areas have direct access from the street side. The walls and floors are pre-cast concrete, and coloured glass polyester is decoratively used for the parts of the building which are not structural.

Ground level entrances to the five-storey housing blocks

View from an inner courtyard (left)

General plan (below)

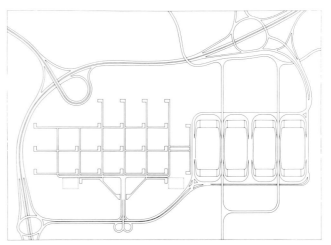

*Walkway on the third level*

# PATRICK HODGKINSON
## Brunswick Centre, Bloomsbury, London (1968–73)

Urban dwelling today provides several choices for different groups of people. This urban scheme, built in the heart of Georgian London by Patrick Hodgkinson, offers a combination of several features in one comprehensive scheme. The basic structure is of two linear terraces containing an open space. The terraces are five to eight storeys high with 560 apartments housing 1644 people. The space between them is divided horizontally on two levels. The lower one is used for storage facilities and parking, the upper one is a pedestrian plaza with a shopping mall. There are 80 shops, a cinema, restaurant and parking for 925 cars. The exterior vertical walls which enclose this grand scheme can also be seen as separating it from the surrounding urban environment.

*General view*

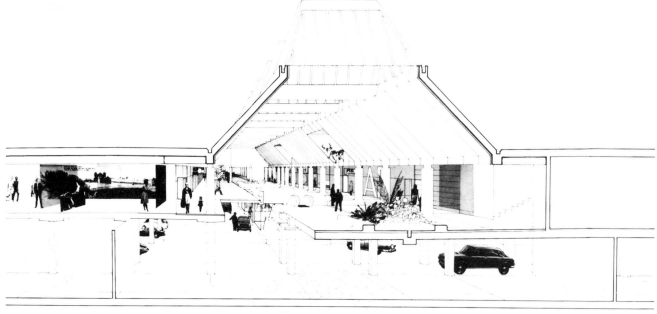

*Shopping hall perspective*

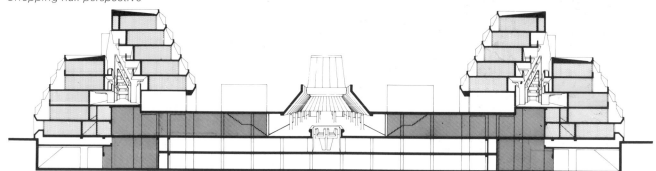

*Cross section*

*O'Donnell Court, one of the apartment blocks at Brunswick Centre*

# RALPH ERSKINE
## Byker Development, Newcastle-upon-Tyne
## (1970–80)

The Byker development scheme in Newcastle-upon-Tyne is one of the best international examples of urban housing to be accepted by the people living in it. It was commissioned in 1968, and construction began in 1970. The aim of the architect was to revitalise parts of the centre of the city of Newcastle. The result is a rather unorthodox scheme for housing on a linear structure with a very complex use of in-between functions such as circulation roads, playgrounds, shopping and social facilities. As a pilot scheme 46 two- and three-storey dwellings were built at Janet Square. The first phase became 'Byker Wall', the perimeter block symbolically protecting the neighbourhood. It is five to eight storeys high, and is made up of flats and maisonettes. The materials used are in-situ concrete and outside brick in various shades of red, brown and yellow. Bedrooms and living rooms face south, overlooking the Byker area; kitchen, bathrooms and storage spaces face north, overlooking the street. The northern windows are few and small. The southern side of the structure has balconies and many large windows. What is achieved is a viable building directed towards participation of the user. Even the architect and several of his collaborators live in the Byker Housing scheme, where they have an architectural office open for consultation with the residents.

*Detail of the south side of the wall (right)*

*North side of the wall*

Ground floor and landscaping plan of Tom Collins House

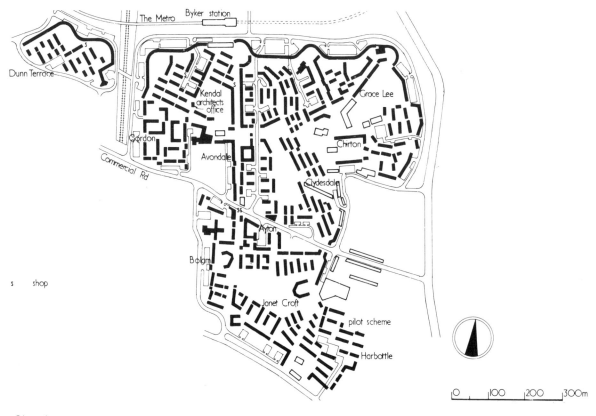

Site plan

32

*South side of the wall*

*Tom Collins house*

33

*Pedestrian walkway at Bowam Coyne*

# Holland

## HERMAN HERTZBERGER
### Central Beheer, Apeldorn
### (1974)

In recent years there have rarely been any new architectural concepts in the design of office buildings in cities. One exception is the office building in Apeldorn by Hertzberger. Here he has managed to combine order and flexibility in complete harmony.

The building is based on a grid-iron plan and structured like a city in small scale. The basic module is a square box approximately 10 × 10 ft, which is arranged in two, three and four storeys. The architect has created spaces which are easily adapted to the different requirements of each working group. The freedom of the individual and the standardisation of the whole are delicately balanced to create an almost domestic atmosphere.

The result is a surprisingly anti-monumental structure, which reveals a clearly anti-hierarchical attitude. The architect expressed it theoretically: 'What we must look for, in place of prototypes which are collective interpretations of individual living patterns, are prototypes which make individual interpretations of the collective patterns possible . . .'

*Working spaces*

*Coffee shop and dining areas*

Aerial view

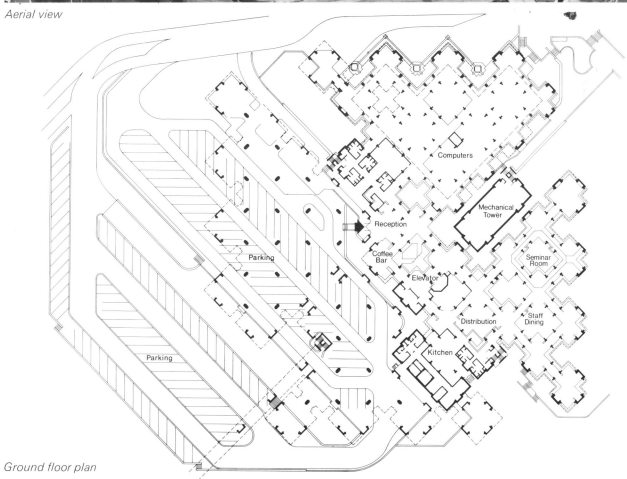

Ground floor plan

Computers

Mechanical
Tower

Reception

Coffee
Bar

Seminar
Room

Elevator

Parking

Distribution

Staff
Dining

Kitchen

Parking

# Germany

## CARLFRIED MUTSCHLER AND PARTNER, JOACHIM LANGNER, DIETER WESSA AND ATELIER WARMBRONN, FREI OTTO, EWALD BUBNER
### Hall, Mannheim
### (1975)

The design in 1973–74 for the Garden Exhibition in Mannheim by Frei Otto, in collaboration with the architects Mutschler and Langner, resulted in a curvilinear shape. This provides an organic environment in which to exhibit flowers. The exterior image of the structure is that of a moulded hill in the landscape. The moulded roof is shaped by a system of wooden lattice-work, which is covered with transparent plastic material. Exterior and interior are separated by a membrane which changes colour according to the intensity of the daylight. Contrary to the earlier tent structures by Frei Otto, which are based on tension, the structure of this wooden equivalent is based on compression.

*The hall by day (opposite) and by night (below)*

*The atmosphere of a park has been created inside the hall*

# HANS DISSING AND OTTO WEITLING
## City Centre, Castrop-Rauxel
## (1971-75)

Based on a limited competition in 1965, in which Alvar Aalto, Egon Eiermann, F. W. Kraemer and Paul Schneider-Esleben participated, Arne Jacobsen and Otto Weitling were awarded the prize. The realisation of the city centre was, after the death of Arne Jacobsen in 1971, continued by Hans Dissing and Otto Weitling, who completed it in 1975.

Castrop-Rauxel is a combination of several communities and has a population of 90,000. The centre consists of a city hall, city auditorium, sports hall, restaurant, adult education building, garage space and an open public plaza (Europaplatz). It is a combination of several administrative and recreational facilities taking an appropriate architectural form. The total concept of the city centre is expressed in the juxtaposition of office towers and the dynamic structures of the sports and civic auditorium with its free span hanging roof of 60·5 yds.

*Council room (right)*

*View of the sports hall and town hall, from the south*

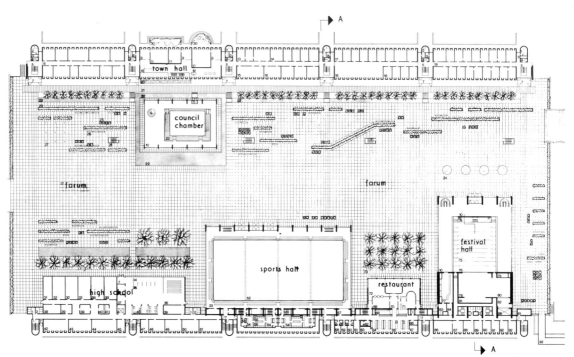

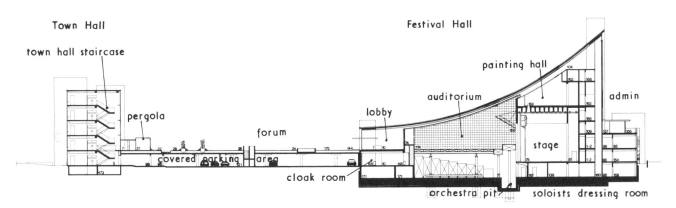

Town Hall

Festival Hall

town hall staircase

painting hall

auditorium

admin

pergola

lobby

forum

stage

covered parking area

cloak room

orchestra pit

soloists dressing room

*Section A-A, showing the festival hall on the right (above)*

*Public plaza with the sports stadium on the right (top)*

*View from courtyard (above left)*

*Ground level plan (left)*

# HARALD DEILMANN
## Old People's Home,
## Porz-Urbach
## (1975–77)

This project won first prize in a competition of 1973 which was commissioned by the Catholic Church community of St Bartholomäus in Porz-Urbach. The complex, built in brick, sandstone and concrete, is organised in two parts: an apartment block and a centre for the care and rehabilitation of old people. The apartments occupy the vertical part of the complex and surround an open courtyard. The low-rise section contains the administrative quarters assembly hall and chapel, and has the character of a village square. This is enhanced by the opportunities to relate outside and inside spaces. The general goal was to integrate the building into the urban fabric, both architecturally and socially.

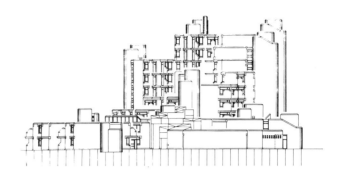

Aerial view showing the whole complex (left)

Apartment blocks (below left)

Section (above)

Meeting area in the rehabilitation centre (below)

*Stairway*

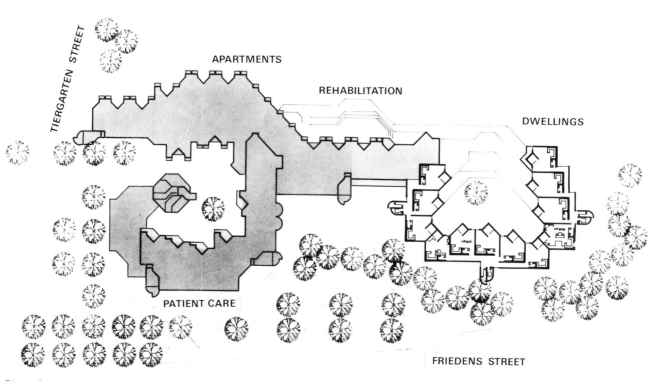

TIERGARTEN STREET

APARTMENTS

REHABILITATION

DWELLINGS

PATIENT CARE

FRIEDENS STREET

*Plan of total complex*

# HANS HOLLEIN
## Municipal Museum Abteiberg, Moenchengladbach
## (1972–78)

The idea of this museum was that it should be integrated into its urban setting. It is surrounded by apartments, youth centre, and high school, all of which have direct access to the museum. The site, which is on a hill, has foot paths and bridges leading into the pedestrian mainstream of city traffic. The museum was built as a space without specific boundaries, giving the user the freedom to relate to either inside or outside. Part of the building's roof is used as terraces and public squares.

The internal organisation of the museum is on two levels, which split into three-storey areas. The area for the permanent collection has approximately 42,000 sq ft and includes a space for temporary exhibitions. Another area is divided into smaller rooms, designed to remain as flexible as possible. A cafeteria has direct access to the garden. There is an audio visual centre, and educational facilities. The administration area, library, and artists' apartments are located in the vertical tower.

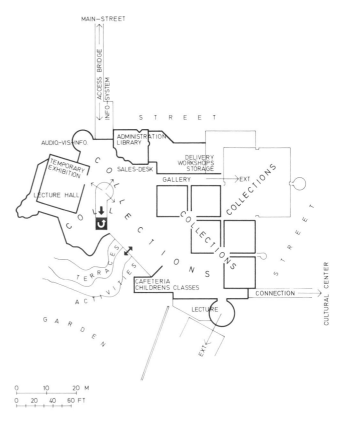

*Ground plan showing main functions (right)*

*Model: view from the south*

47

*Model: view from the terraced garden*

*Model: view showing the roof terrace (right) and main entrance (centre)*

*Section*

48

# France

## MICHEL ANDRAULT AND PIERRE PARAT
### Caisse Régionale de Crédit Agricole, Orléans
### (1972–73)

The complex of the central offices and social facilities of the Caisse Régionale de Crédit Agricole in Orléans is based on the principle of seven large rectangular two-storey pavilions which are connected by circular vertical circulation towers and surround an interior open courtyard. In principle, it is a variation of Louis I. Kahn's Philadelphia laboratories with its separation of servant and served spaces. Under the central courtyard is an assembly hall with a seating capacity of 250. The vertical circular towers are in reinforced concrete, the façades of the office blocks have aluminium elements and tinted glass.

*Detail of façade*

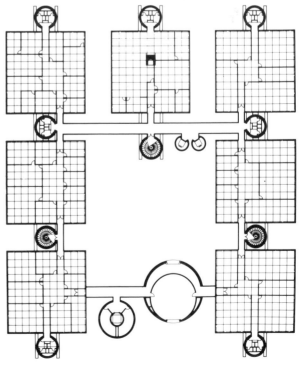

*Plan showing the seven rectangular pavilions and circular connecting towers*

*View from the central courtyard*

*Main entrance*

Sculptured garden

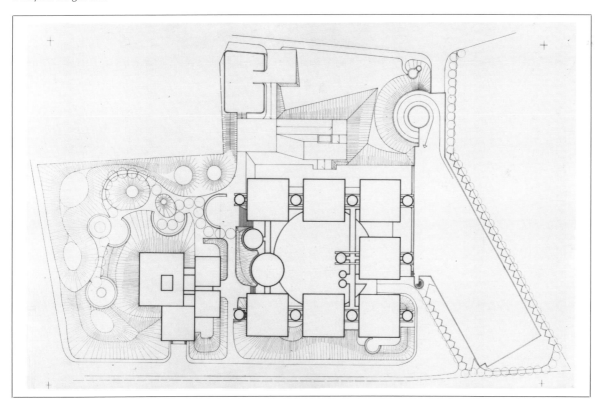

Site plan

## PIANO AND ROGERS
## Centre Pompidou, Paris
## (1971–76)

The Centre National d'Art et de Culture Georges Pompidou was authorised by government legislation in 1975. The idea of Centre Pompidou was the creation of a multi-purpose centre in the old market area of Paris which combined facilities for information, education and entertainment. Part of the Centre is a museum of modern art with 20,500 sq yds devoted to permanent exhibition plus 24,300 sq yds for temporary exhibitions. The rest of the building consists of a centre for Industrial Creation, a public information library, the Institut de Recherche et de Coordination Acoustique/Musique, a restaurant and a public square. The architects Renzo Piano and Richard Rogers, who won first prize in an international competition, aimed at creating a flexible space for people rather than a cultural monument for the élite.

The building is bound by public squares. The main one lies west of the building and there are two smaller squares, one to the south and the other south-west of the building. The main plaza slopes down approximately 3 yds towards the structure. The building, which has no formal façade, is composed of a structural system of 48 steel beams resting on steel supports. This framework contains five floors, each 53 × 187 yds. These enormous spaces are completely flexible internally. Underground there are three levels of parking. The ground floor was built as a large public forum, 1368 sq yds and 16 yds high. This is the area for entertainment and the general information centre. The circulation system is on the west side and consists of vertical elevations, horizontal corridors and diagonal escalators, which are openly visible. A restaurant on the top floor provides an excellent view over the city of Paris.

Entrance hall (left)

Night view (below, left)

View over Paris from a pedestrian gallery (below)

*West façade with external escalators and connecting galleries*

*Exposed services on the east façade showing the air-handling units of the roof and air-conditioning ducts leading from them*

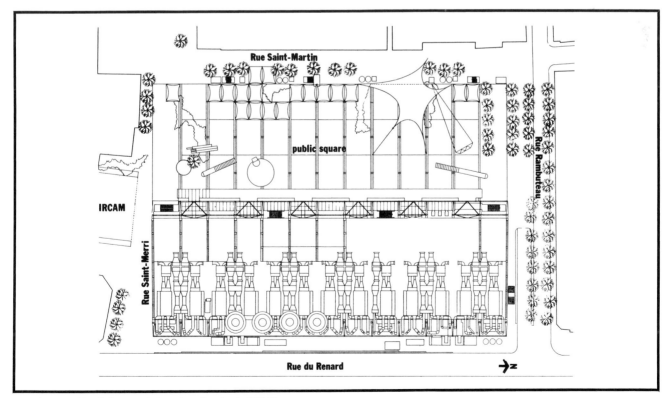

*Roof plan of building and site plan (scale 1:1500)*

# Switzerland

## ATELIER 5
## Thalmatt Housing, Herrenschwanden (1972–74)

Atelier 5's first experiment in housing based on ownership in a communal environment was in Halen. They then made another attempt to create this harmony in Thalmatt Housing, northwest of Halen. Preparations go back as far as 1967, building began in August 1972, and by September 1974 all houses were sold and occupied.

On a site of 8910 sq yds there are 22 houses of different sizes, some as large as 8 rooms, and some with two apartments. The units are on two levels, the upper units with three storeys, the lower with two storeys, on both sides of a pedestrian street which is partially covered. All car traffic is excluded. The arrangement follows that of the hill-site plan in Halen, using a slope for the terraced houses. The result is a cluster of one-family houses.

The houses are individually owned and the participation of the owner during the planning phase of the interior arrangement was of great significance for the outcome of the project. The cost ranges from 200,000 to 670,000 Swiss francs, according to the size of the house. As in Halen, the Thalmatt architects were able to prove that individuality and communication in contemporary housing is possible on a realistic basis.

*The central court on opening day (right)*

*The south-west corner of the housing scheme (below)*

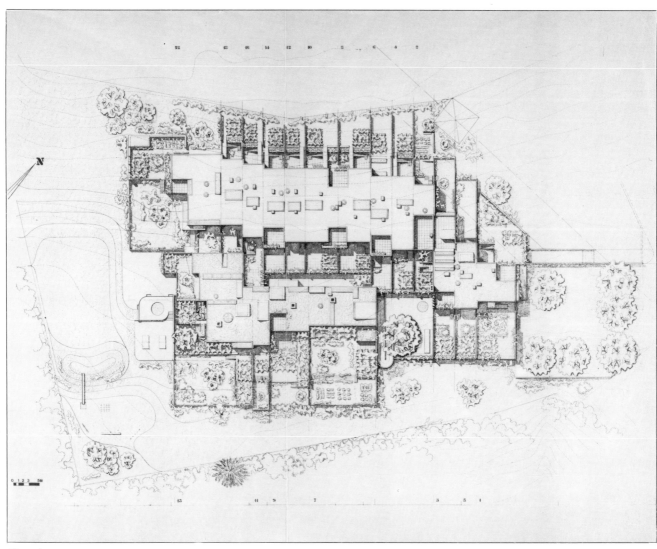

*Site plan*

*View from the north*

# MARIO BOTTA
## School, Morbio Inferiore
## (1972–76)

This secondary school in the south of Switzerland is one of the outstanding examples of school buildings in recent years. The architect has harmoniously integrated the school into the landscape of the valley, and at the same time created an independent and stimulating architectural environment.

This school consists of eight units in a linear arrangement, each with four classrooms on the ground floor for general use and four rooms on the floor above for specific subjects. Botta has designed his space differently on each floor; in this way the function of each floor is clearly stated. The classroom wing is thus seen as one coherent linear space for circulation on the ground floor, and divides into separate clusters on the first floor. A wing for sports activities at the end of the classroom block was completed in 1977. The open space is arranged in such a way as to create an open-air theatre with varying levels which can be used as seating.

*Main entrance*

*Stairway to the top level*

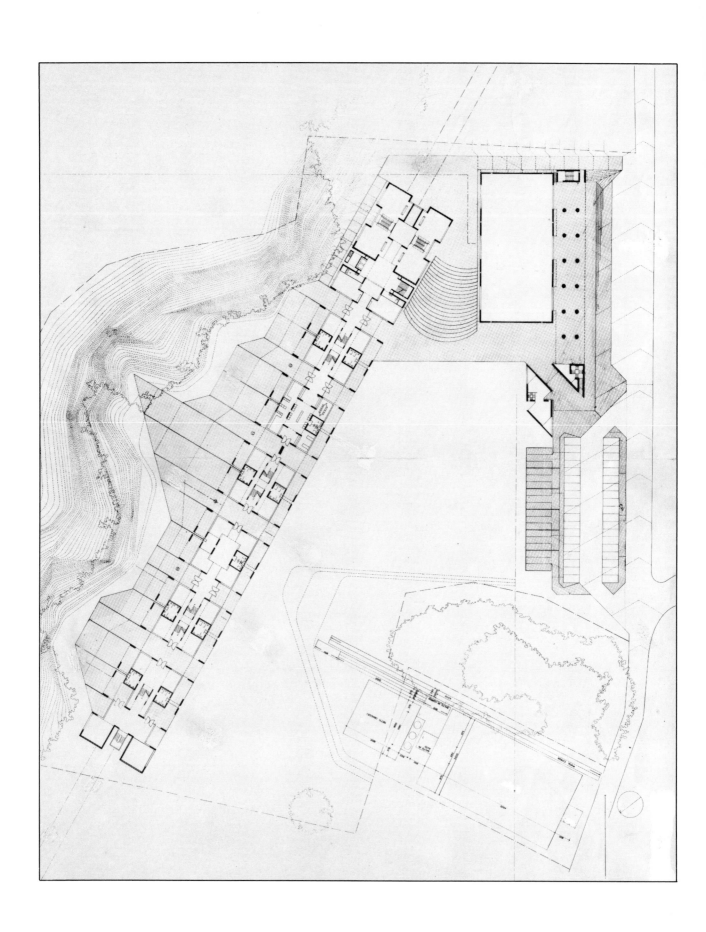

Site plan

*The school in its valley setting*

*Parking facilities for the schoolchildren's bicycles*

# Liechtenstein

**RICARDO PORRO**
**Art Centre, Vaduz**
**(1969–75)**

This small privately owned art centre in Vaduz was designed by the revolutionary Cuban architect Porro, who now lives in Paris. It consists of a private office for the client, a museum for his art collection and additional office space in the basement for rent. The building, on a mountain site over Vaduz, is based on the juxtaposition of square and curved forms. The curves extend into a structure of hanging vertical columns which wrap around the building like a transparent veil. Scaled to human size, the structure contrasts two materials, one heavy and opaque, the other light and mobile. The symbolism of the materials, gold and aluminium, incorporates the gold of the Nibelungs, the alchemy of Paracelsus and German financial investments in Liechtenstein. The result is tension and movement; the architect is attempting to free the building from the static of architectural form, and at the same time to express the ambivalence of fire and knowledge, gold and light. The three floors of the interior are arranged in a sequence of curvilinear ways. This gives a sense of continuous space.

*The interior stairway*

*Detail of the façade (right)*

62

*General view*

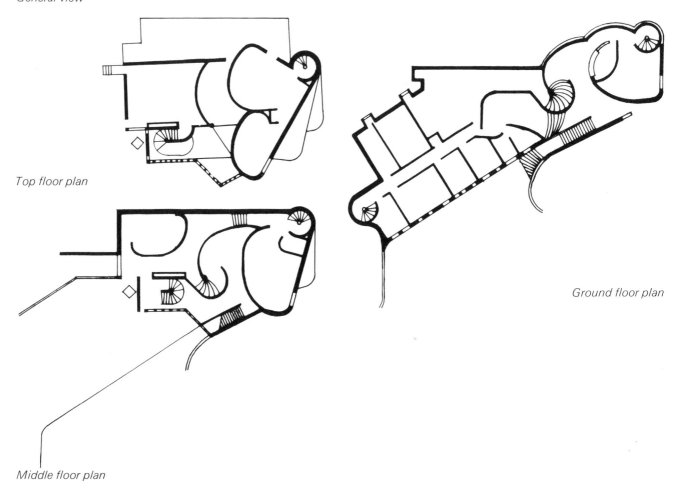

*Top floor plan*

*Middle floor plan*

*Ground floor plan*

Italy

## GIANCARLO DE CARLO
**Matteotti Village in Terni**
**(1971–74)**

The concept of Giancarlo de Carlo's work is directed towards an architecture into which the user has a greater input than is usual. His work can be seen as a reaction against those developments of the modern movement which actually decreased the participation of people who are subjected to the changing fashions of the individual architect. De Carlo collaborated on the building plans with the 250 workers of the Societa Terni, an iron mill in Terni, for whom the housing was intended. De Carlo was commissioned to build the project in 1969, but because of varying degrees of cooperation by the client the housing was not completed until 1974. The low-rise high density housing is penetrated with green areas for an optimum of user participation. There are 45 alternatives in the 250 unit housing complex, which take into consideration the individual demands towards better community interaction.

**GIANCARLO DE CARLO**
**Matteotti Village in Terni**
*Buildings either side of the street are bridged by walkways*

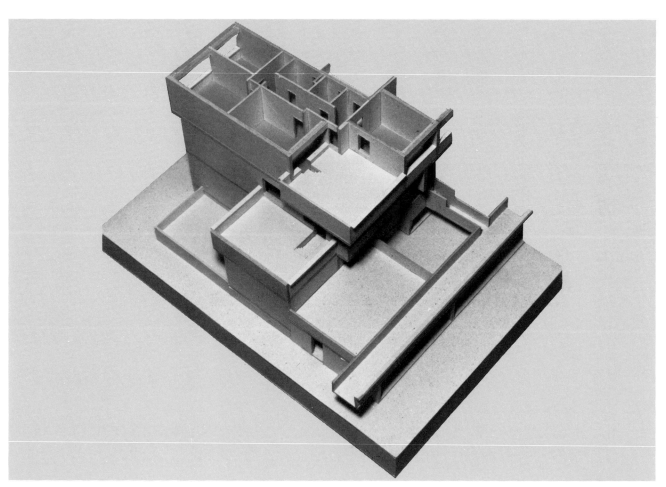

66

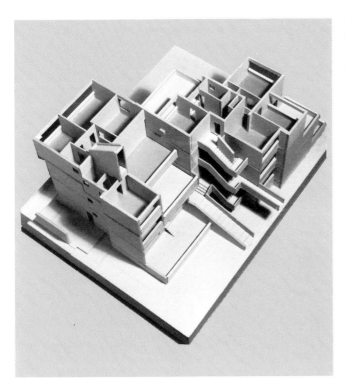

Two of the models prepared by the architects to show different
housing types (left and far left)

View along one of the main access roads (below left)

Site plan (below)

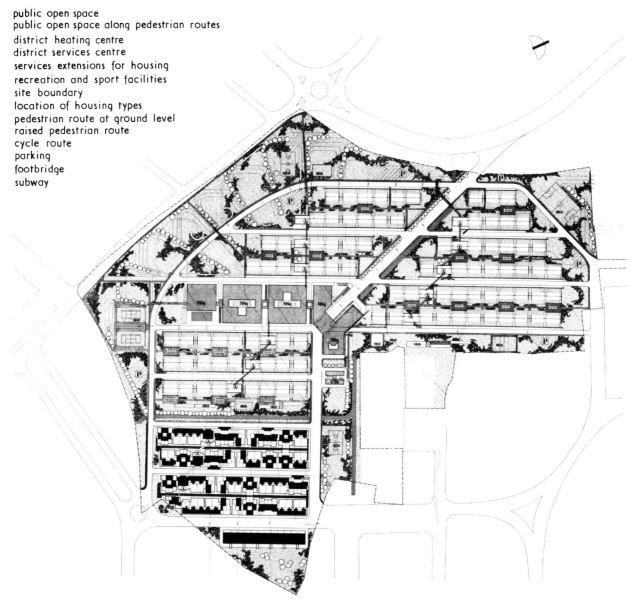

public open space
public open space along pedestrian routes
district heating centre
district services centre
services extensions for housing
recreation and sport facilities
site boundary
location of housing types
pedestrian route at ground level
raised pedestrian route
cycle route
parking
footbridge
subway

# VITTORIO GREGOTTI
## Textile Factory, Rovellasca
## (1972)

This industrial complex is designed in an open-ended low square 'slab' which allows for future expansion. The vertical structure is a system of modules, 33 × 33 ft, in reinforced concrete. On one side of the one-storey square is an elevated linear structure accentuated by a vaulted roof. This area, housing management and commercial offices, computer and exhibition space, has a special lighting system visible from the outside, which gives structure to the lower parts of the building.

*General plan (below)*

*Front and side elevations of the building (bottom)*

*The offices of the factory are in the area spanned by the vaulted roof (right, below)*

*Main entrance (opposite)*

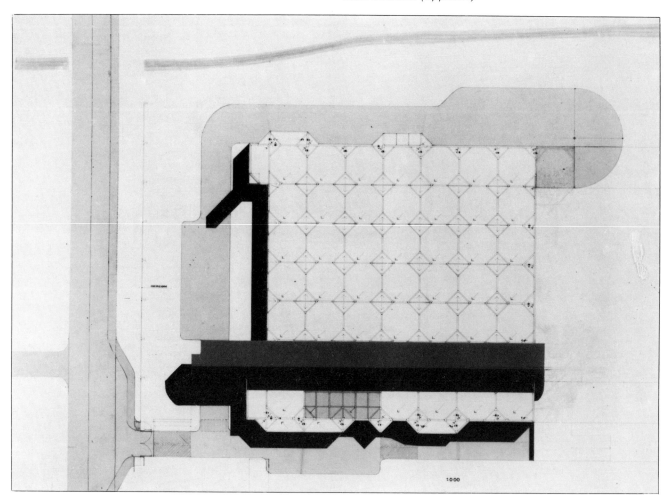

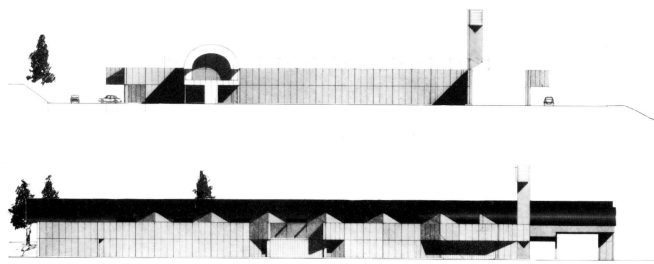

# ALDO ROSSI
## Housing, Gallaratese, Milan
## (1965–70)

The work of Aldo Rossi is one of the fundamental contributions to contemporary architecture. The housing complex in Gallaratese, built in collaboration with Carlo Aymonino, is one of the most radical examples. It is not by chance that Rossi deals with low-cost high-density housing, as it is considered the most crucial building-type challenge to present-day architects. Rossi takes into consideration the city, the site and earlier architectural manifestations as part of the design for his housing. History is therefore an integral element in his contemporary design. Rossi's block of housing is 600 ft long and 40 ft wide, and is part of a larger scheme in an urban environment. The relation towards the open urban space is articulated by porticos and arcades, which are defined spaces for human interaction. Street and building are integrated in the tradition of old architecture in Milan.

*Detail of an entrance and stairs to the apartments (below)*

*Exterior view of the entrance (right)*

*View of the residential block (right, below)*

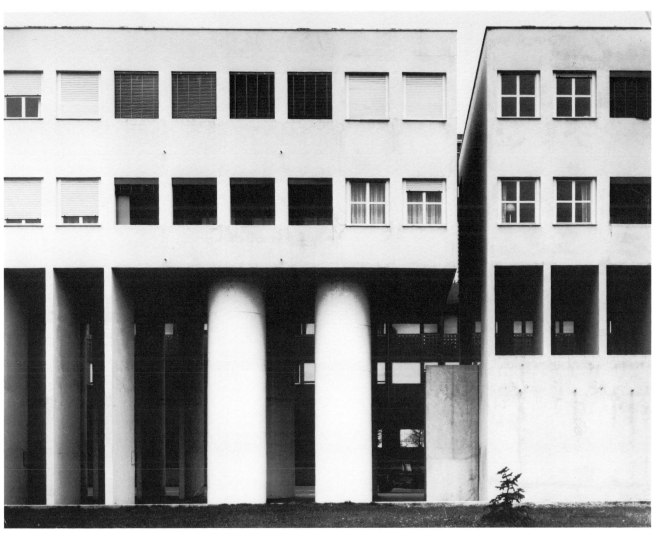

*Interior view of the entrance*

## CAPPAI AND MAINARDIS
## Olivetti Social and Residential Centre, Ivrea
## (1967–74)

This complex is a residential and social centre for the employees of the Olivetti factory. Due to excavations of Roman and medieval ruins on the site, the building had to be slightly altered in the course of construction. In its completed form it consists of a residential area with 55 apartments (one- and two-bedroom) which is operated as a hotel. There is a social centre below the apartments with cultural facilities, a swimming pool, snack bar, and restaurant, all open to the people of the city of Ivrea. Based on prefabricated construction and the use of concrete and metal in the exterior skin of the structure, the building constitutes a new type of industrial architecture, defining services to workers in a new architectural articulation.

*Detail showing the exterior metal skin (right)*

*Front view showing the domed social centre with apartments behind*

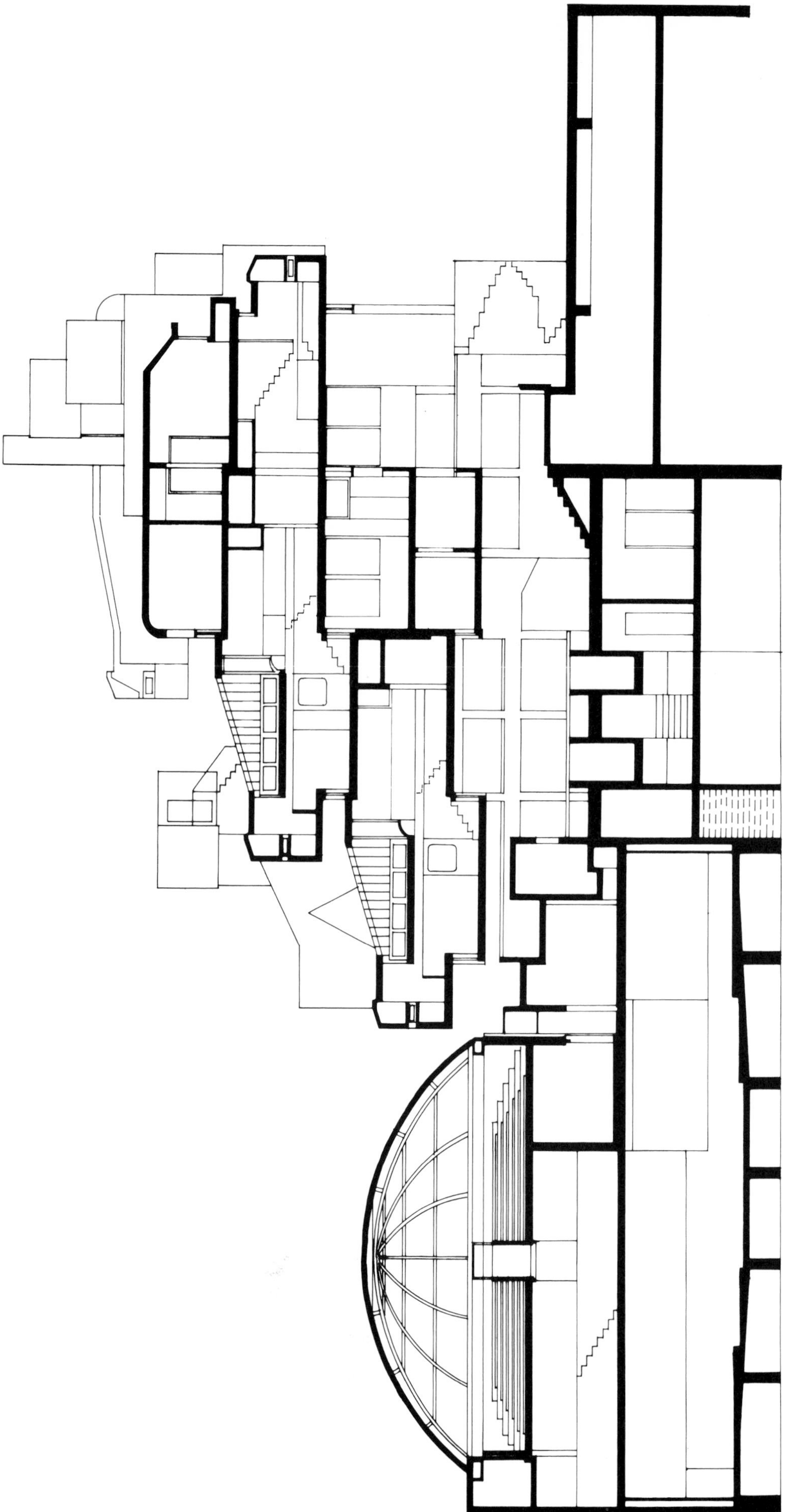

Section

*The side entrance*

*The top of the apartment block*

# Spain

## JULIO CANO LASSO AND ALBERTO CAMPO BAEZA
### Technical University, Almeria
### (1974)

The architecture of the new Technical University of Almeria is in harmony with the tradition and conditions of the site. The campus is located outside the city of Almeria and is composed of simple elementary forms, with white walls and open spaces. There is a contrast between the fortress-like exterior, which is in line with the traditional architectural elements of the region, and the friendly atmosphere of the internal space with its open courtyards and gardens. There are 22 gardens on the campus.

The school is organised on a modular grid of 13 × 13 ft and two axes which cross in the centre, creating an open piazza for meetings and interaction among the academic community. To the north of the centre is the main entrance to the university, the library and administration, to the south is the cafeteria and kitchen. East of the piazza are the classrooms, studios and laboratories, and to the west the student dormitories. Every part of the university is easily accessible. Construction was simple and did not take long to build. It is seen as incomplete by the architect as the trees have not yet reached maturity, and changes are to be expected as the institution expands.

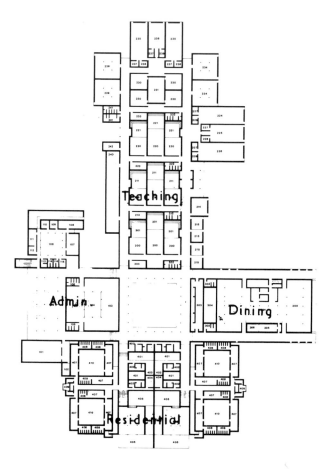

General plan (above)

Central courtyard (above, right)

Exterior view (right)

Plants overhanging the stark, fortress-like walls (right)

The lounge in one of the residences (below)

The walls form massive cubes

Finland

## REIMA PIETILAE
## Suvikumpi Housing, Tapiola
## (1969–70)

Pietilae participated in a competition arranged by Asuntosa-eaetio in 1962 and was awarded the first prize. The project was built in 1969–1970. The scheme consists of 140 apartments in a large continuous complex of different heights from 2 to 9 storeys following a linear pattern. It has been designed into the forest landscape of Tapiola. The Finnish name Suvikumpi means 'summer hill' and the scheme captures the atmosphere of summer and vacation. The first part of the housing scheme, named Suvikulma, was completed in 1967. A second part was completed in 1968, called Suvikeskus, the last part was completed in 1970, called Suvikaerki.

*General views showing the way in which the building design echoes the form and markings Tof the birch trees which surround it (above and top right)*

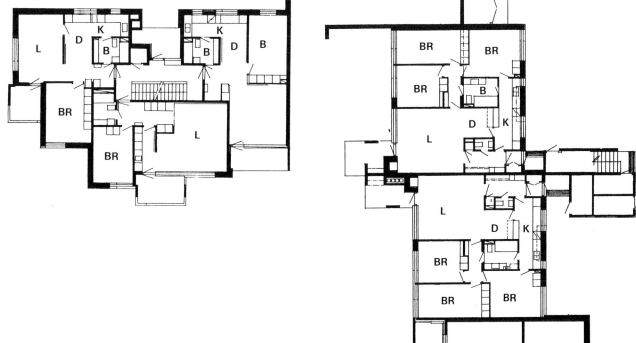

*Layouts of individual apartments*

## KARI VIRTA
## Oulu University, Oulu
## (1971–  )

This project for a university in the arctic climate of northern Finland was given first prize in a competition held in 1967–68. The building plan was divided into three phases; the first phase was completed in 1973, the second in 1976.

The university is built to accommodate 7,000 students and the campus is located about five kilometres from the centre of the town. The planning scheme is based on one to four storey linear buildings extending from the main building in the central section, which contains an assembly hall, restaurants, a café, lounges and exhibition space. These buildings are characterised by an exterior skin of enamelled aluminium sheets in bright primary colours. A pedestrian circulation links all the different departments of the university. Emphasis is placed on the inter-relationships of the educational facilities as an expression of the inter-disciplinary concept. In addition to classrooms and social facilities, housing for approximately 3,000 students has been planned.

*The library*

*A student seminar in progress (below)*

*Courtyard landscaping*

*Lounge and eating areas*

84

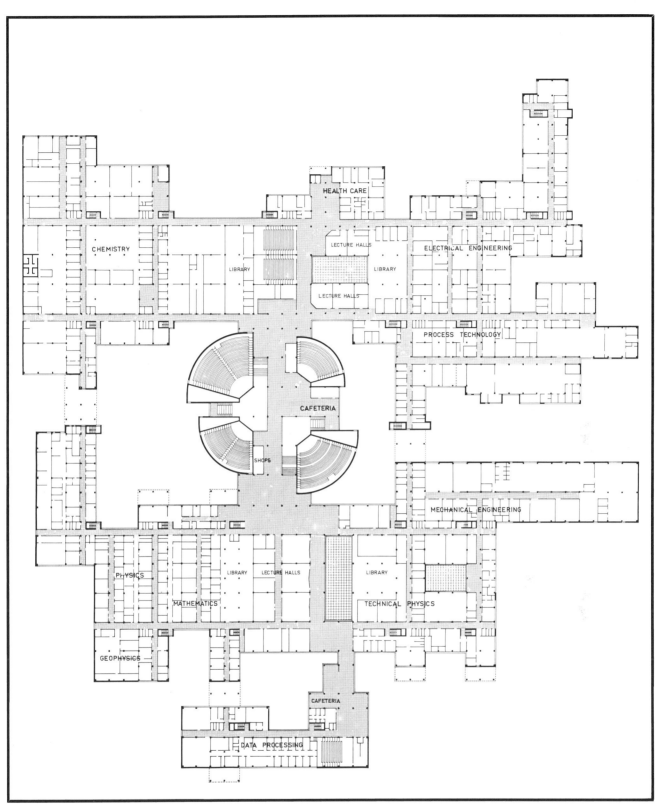

*General plan*

Czechoslovakia

## ATELIER SIAL
### Department Store Maj, Prague
### (1975)

The site chosen for the Department Store Maj is on the corner of one of the most frequented streets in the central part of the city. The building consists of two sections, one seven storeys high, the other four. The three upper storeys with their curved glass windows dominate the shape of the building. Three levels below the ground floor contain engine rooms, workshops and a supermarket. The four main floors above ground are sales rooms which have great flexibility of space. The fifth floor has a restaurant, kitchen and refreshment rooms. The sixth floor contains offices and a canteen for the employees, and the top floor is reserved for the computer and engine functions. A ramp leads to parking space on two levels of the roof over the four-storey section of the building. The entire structure is of prefabricated precast concrete and the cladding of pre-fabricated concrete panels and enamelled aluminium panels.

*View from the street*

*Escalators inside the building (opposite)*

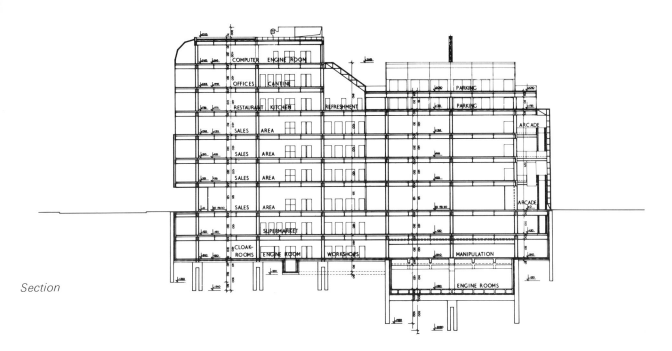

Section

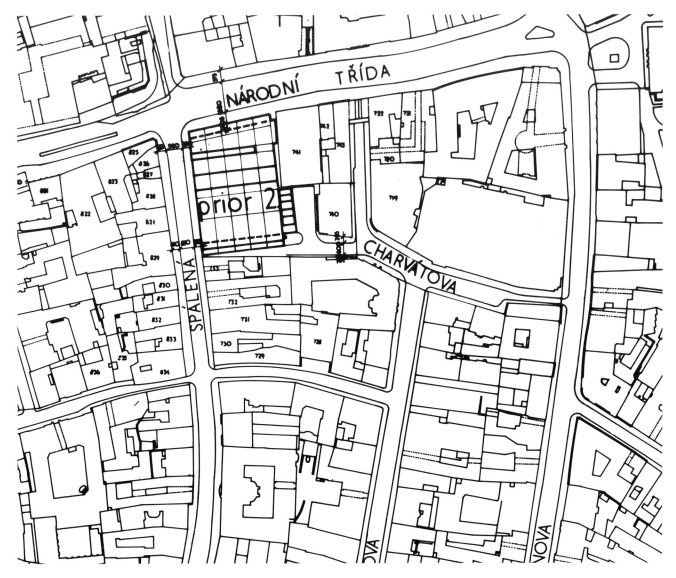

Site plan (above)

Model of the store (left)

89

# Hungary

## GYOERGY KÉVÉS
## Housing, Budapest
## (1976–77)

In recent years East European architects have excelled in innovative ideas, especially in the field of industrialisation. These technological innovations were often developed within the framework of large state companies, such as Iparterv in Budapest, for which Kévés developed a light steel structural system. As a private designer Kévés, in collaboration with his wife Eva Foeldvari, built several housing estates, which culminated in the structure on XI Zolyomi Street in Budapest 44 A/B, built in 1976–77. A hilly site was chosen for the housing scheme, which is in two blocks, each four storeys in height. The blocks are in terraces on the hillside.

The two stepped apartment blocks in terraces on the hillside

Each apartment has a garden, rather like a balcony (left, above)

The second stepped apartment block on the hillside (left)

*Outside stairways on the second block of apartments*

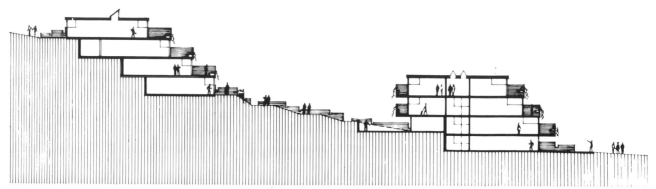

*Section*

USSR

## ILIA CHERNIAVSKII, I. POPOV AND I. VASILEVSKII
### Trade union holiday hotel, Voronovo (1974)

The building at Vornovo was designed by a team of architects and engineers from the Central Research Institute for the Experimental Design of Leisure Buildings, whose Director is A. T. Polianskii. Located 60 km from Moscow, it is an example of the *dom otdykha* (literally 'home of rest'), a building type receiving increasing attention in the Soviet Union now as part of the general policy of improving leisure facilities.

In this complex and their others elsewhere in the USSR, it is the team's principle (as Cherniavskii has written) 'to use the landscape's own characteristic compositional devices within the buildings as a means of switching the individual off from his everyday world', to maximise the therapeutic effectiveness of visits, however short. Whilst the visual rhythms and modes of spatial organisation are thus 'contrasted to those of urban housing', clever exploitation of selected precast concrete components from Moscow Region's standard housing systems made it possible at Voronovo to provide an exceptionally wide range of facilities within the normal cost limits for this building type.

The main sculptural block contains the public facilities, assembled on three floors around the foyers of a dramatically top-lit central staircase. They include a 720-seat auditorium; a sports hall; bars; dancing areas; library and reading room; bowling alley; billiard room; television rooms; an exhibition gallery. A subtley fragmented 560-seat restaurant gives ground-level landscape views, and an indoor swimming pool runs out under it towards the lake.

Balconied 1–3 person suites for the 560 guests form a four-storied 'tail' running between the lakeshore and the pine forests, oriented for maximum year-round sun penetration. Lifts and stairs connect at ground level with a linear winter garden, along which are located paramedical facilities, hairdressers, Post Office and shops.

Throughout the building the maximum use has been made of natural materials, in particular travertine and timbers, with bold colour complements to the landscape outside provided by planting and furnishings. Windows are anodised aluminium. External walls are clad in Azerbaidzhanyi travertine. The structure of the main block is a 9 m x 12 m steel frame with concrete floors; the bedroom wing has a 7·2 m grid of crosswalls.

*The north-east corner: the main mass of the sports hall with restaurant terrace and swimming pool below, where the water level is raised to give the sensation of swimming in an extension of the lake beyond*

93

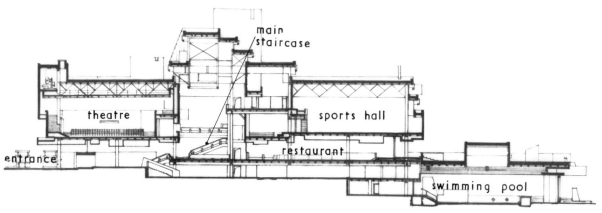

*A view across the central staircase hall (left) at the level of the sports hall spectators' gallery. A vast copper light-fitting pierces downwards through several floors from the rooflight structure above*

*Section A—A (below left, see plan overleaf)*

*Looking inland from the south-east corner of the roof terrace (right) with one corner of the restaurant under the sports hall to the right, and the bedroom wing running off to the left in the background*

*Then new Voronovo complex from the south-east (below) where the small original leisure home in a converted country mansion is connected to the new one by a footbridge over the lake*

Garden entrance from the lake side (above)
with main block of public facilities to the
right and bedroom wing to the left

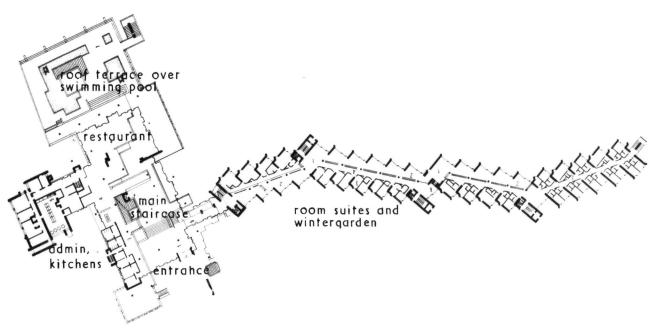

Plan at entrance and restaurant level

Mexico

## FERNANDO GONZALES GORTAZAR
### Commercial Centre 'Mexicana Americas', Guadalajara
### (1976–77)

The combination of various functions in urban structures has been gaining world-wide importance and the Commercial Centre 'Mexicana Americas' in Guadalajara by the young Mexican architect Fernando Gonzalez Gortazar is an example of this building type. Located in the centre of the city and filling a city block measuring 109 × 64 m, the building contains four levels which integrate its various functions into the vital core of urban life. The lowest level, which is underground, is mainly used as a parking lot, but it also houses service functions as well as a small cinema which is entered from the street level. An intermediate level which is 2 m under the street level contains shops and other commercial facilities. There are staircases connecting the shopping level to the parking garage below and the street level above. The third, and main, level, is above the street level and is occupied by a supermarket which can be entered from all other levels by means of escalators, lifts or ramps. The fourth, and highest, level contains the supermarket storerooms and offices. The aim of the architect was to vertically connect the different storeys and create a spatial unity which is accentuated by works of art such as sculptures, fountains and reliefs.

*Detail showing the gargoyle-like concrete containers which are part of an extensive drainage network designed to cope with heavy rainstorms*

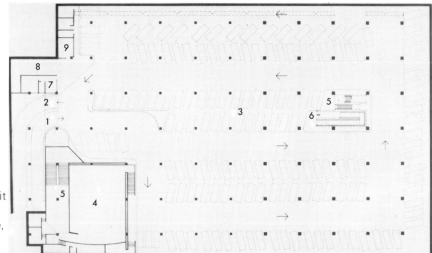

*Basement plan:* 1—Entrance ramp, 2—Exit ramp, 3—Parking area, 4—Cinema, 5—Stairs up, 6—Ramp up, 7—Security office, 8—Machine room (electric system), 9—Machine room (hydraulic system)

*A large vertical space contains the ramp and escalator linking the intermediate and main levels (above)*

*Interior of the intermediate level: roof design of grey and white zig-zag stripes, floor of blue enamelled ceramic, and red metallic sculpture designed by the architect (opposite)*

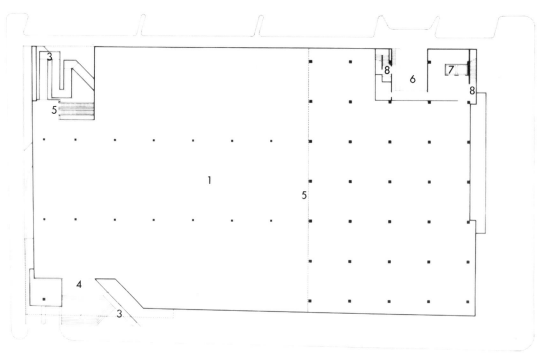

*Main floor plan*: 1—Supermarket sales area, 2—Escalator down, 3—Ramp, 4—Stairs to street, 5—Projection of level change (limit of storeroom), 6—Goods unloading, 7—Goods lift (up to storeroom), 8—Stairs (up to storeroom)

*The main entrance. All façades of the building are clad in specially designed textured concrete panels*

# Argentina

## MANTEOLA, SANCHEZ, GOMEZ, SANTOS, SOLSONA AND VINOLY
### Colour Television Production Centre, Buenos Aires
### (1978–79)

The hybrid character of architectural tasks since 1970 is well illustrated by this television centre which integrates high electronic technology on a multi-purpose site. Working against a tight deadline the architects had to design and build the centre in time to broadcast the 1978 soccer finals. One of the most efficient television centres in the world, it contains 265,000 square feet of complicated facilities, including 7 sound proof studios. The largest studio, which contains 400 seats, is also used for public performances and had to have a separate entrance. The architects built the centre under a roof which they designed to be used as a public plaza extending to the adjacent park. Through this solution the architects returned large parts of the park site on which the building was constructed by designing a public area which includes playgrounds, a public ampitheatre and entertainment facilities. Great care was taken by the architects to design two separate parts, the functional units inside the television centre and the public parts on top of it, in an inter-relatedness which brings new dimension to 'underground architecture'.

*View of the public plaza*

*Diagonal window (above)*

*Plaza (left)*

*Entrance lobby (below)*

*Exterior of one of the studios (right)*

*Television studios and public plaza (below, right)*

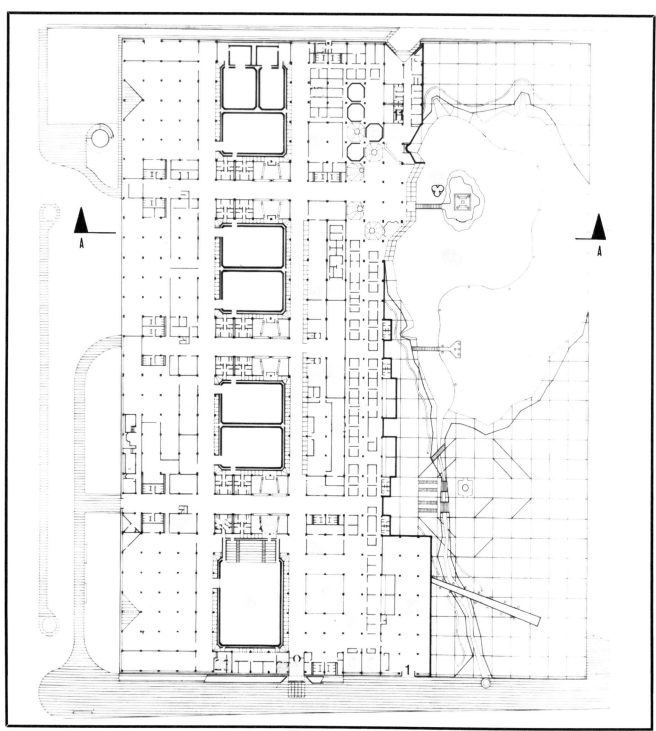

Ground floor plan

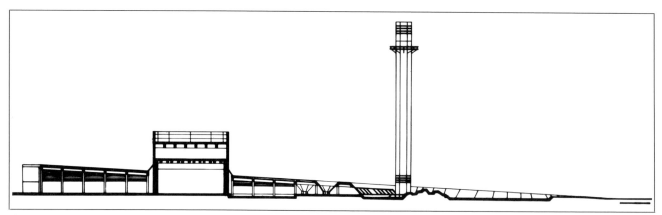

Section AA

104

# Peru

## TOIVO KORHONEN
### Housing, Lima
### (1975–76)

In a competition in 1969 the United Nations invited architects to design prototypes for low-cost housing. The participating architects were James Stirling, Charles Correa, Kiyonori Kikutake, Noriaki Kurokawa, Christopher Alexander, Giancarlo de Carlo, Atelier 5, Herbert Ohl, Aldo van Eyck, Oskar Hansen and Toivo Korhonen, presenting a wealth of ideas in response to the most difficult challenge to architecture today. One of the many architects contributing to the low-cost housing situation in Lima is the Finnish architect Toivo Korhonen. His project consists of two housing blocks which together total 21 one-family houses and are part of a larger community of 500 houses. The size of the housing blocks vary between 48 and 97 sq yds, and can eventually be extended up to 238 yds. A modular grid laid as the base is approximately 12 × 12 ft, and the structural frame is in accordance with these measurements. Materials for the structural frame are prefabricated concrete in skeleton construction and are earthquake resistant. The main construction remained within traditional methods, which was mostly masonry by hand. A certain number of houses were left half finished so they could be completed by the owner.

*Street elevation of the pre-fabricated version of the house*

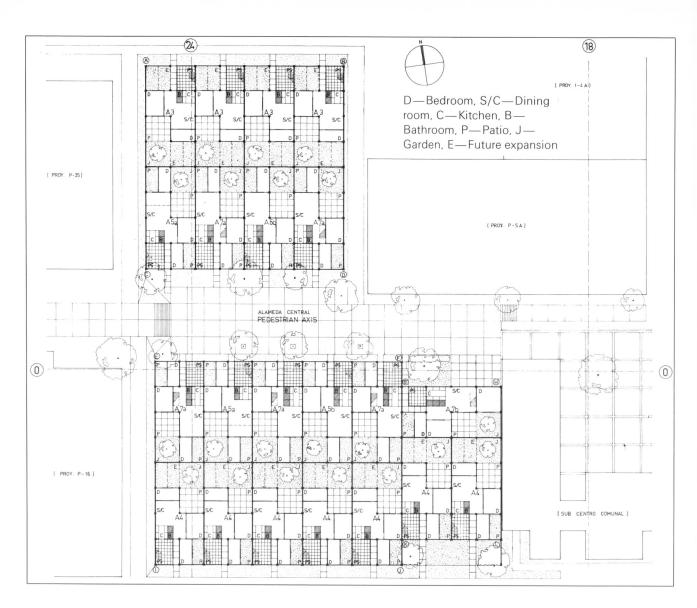

N

D—Bedroom, S/C—Dining room, C—Kitchen, B—Bathroom, P—Patio, J—Garden, E—Future expansion

ALAMEDA CENTRAL
PEDESTRIAN AXIS

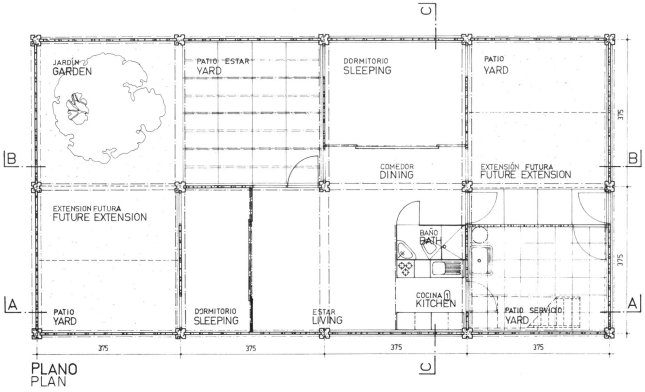

JARDÍN
GARDEN

PATIO ESTAR
YARD

DORMITORIO
SLEEPING

PATIO
YARD

375

B

COMEDOR
DINING

EXTENSIÓN FUTURA
FUTURE EXTENSION

B

EXTENSIÓN FUTURA
FUTURE EXTENSION

BAÑO
BATH

375

A

PATIO
YARD

DORMITORIO
SLEEPING

ESTAR
LIVING

COCINA 1
KITCHEN

PATIO SERVICIO
YARD

A

375          375          375          375

PLANO
PLAN

*Ground floor plan of the complete scheme (opposite, above)*
*General view of the main, pedestrian street of the community*
*(left)*
*Street elevation of the masonry version of the house (above,*
*top)*
*Plan of a two-bedroom house (above)*

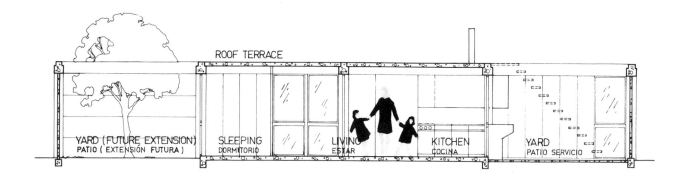

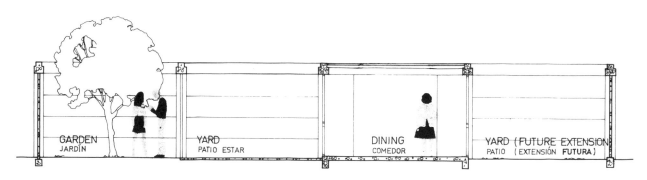

Sections A-A (above) and B-B (below) of the two-bedroom
house

The opposite side of the main street (see photograph on
page 106)

Morocco

## ABDESLEM FARAOUI AND PATRICE DE MAZIÈRES
### Hotel, Boumalne du Dades
### (1976)

The earlier phases of architecture in Morocco were strongly influenced by the French tradition. In recent years, however, there has been a strong awareness of the local tradition in building design, which relates to local topography and history. This hotel by Faraoui and de Mazières is one among many of their buildings where the structure is in line with the cubic modular building forms of the old Islamic architecture in the region. The architects have created self-contained living accommodation in a hostile environment resembling an old fortress by combining pyramidal shapes and cubical form.

*View of the patio and swimming pool*

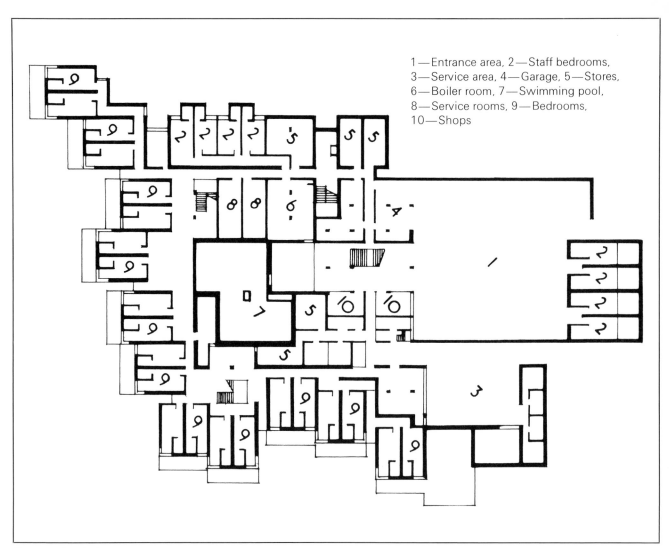

1—Entrance area, 2—Staff bedrooms,
3—Service area, 4—Garage, 5—Stores,
6—Boiler room, 7—Swimming pool,
8—Service rooms, 9—Bedrooms,
10—Shops

*Entrance level plan*

*Interior view with the dining room beyond*

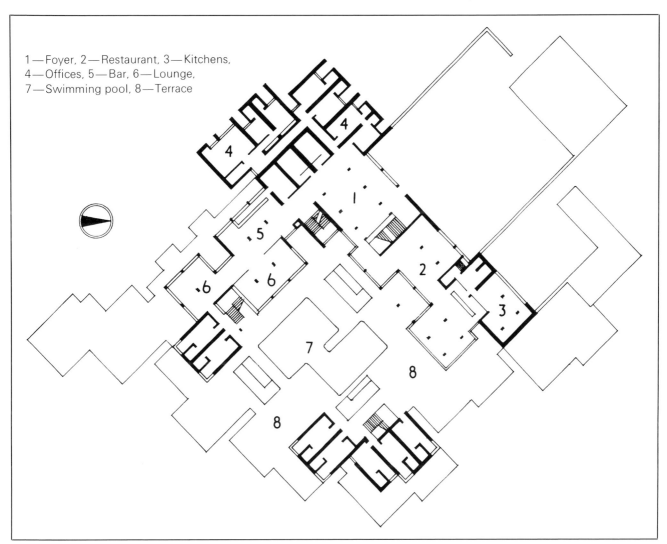

1—Foyer, 2—Restaurant, 3—Kitchens,
4—Offices, 5—Bar, 6—Lounge,
7—Swimming pool, 8—Terrace

*Upper level plan*

*General view*

View from the north-west (right)

General view (below)

Section (bottom)

112

# Zambia

## MONTGOMERIE, OLDFIELD AND KIRBY
### Bank of Zambia staff maisonettes, Lusaka (1971)

Housing in Africa is still in the first phase of experimentation. Slowly changing from foreign imports to local identity, every step of its architecture is directed towards a new and fuller understanding of the country's own way of life. One of these steps can be seen in the maisonettes for the staff of the bank of Zambia in Lusaka. Located on the corner of Shakespeare Road and Independence Avenue, the project contains 12 two-bedroom, 11 four-bedroom and 6 three-bedroom dwellings which in their interrelated design form a compact unit. Three separate blocks surround an open grassy centre space in which there is a service area and playground. Each dwelling has a small patio which is closed off from the public space by a curved honeycombed screen wall. Alongside the wall is the entrance to the dwelling. The kitchen is on the ground floor level and serves the adjacent living/dining area. A stairway leads to the upper storey where the bedrooms are located. The dominating material is brick which was given a refined sculptural quality in the screens and in addition is accentuated by large round openings which offer an in-between space on the second and third floor levels.

*View from the city*

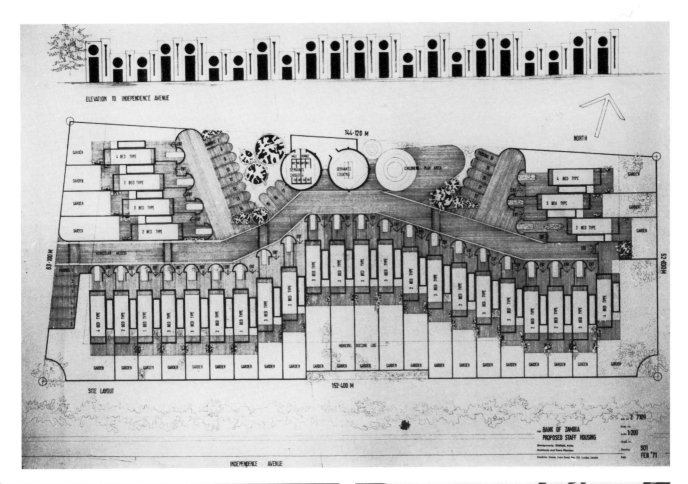

ELEVATION TO INDEPENDENCE AVENUE

NORTH

144·120 M

SITE LAYOUT

152·400 M

INDEPENDENCE AVENUE

BANK OF ZAMBIA
PROPOSED STAFF HOUSING

501
FEB '71

The inner court from the west (above)

Site plan and elevation (top)

Typical units seen from the inner court (opposite, above)

The inner court looking across the soft play area (left)

# Israel

## ZVI HECKER
## Ramot Housing, Jerusalem
## (1972–78)

The housing project in Ramot, commissioned by the Ministry of Housing in Israel, is about 3 miles from the centre of the city on a hilly site and covers an area of approximately 70 acres. Its first phase consists of 720 residential units arranged in a layout resembling the shape of a hand with five branch-like fingers. In the centre is a community area consisting of shopping and administration facilities. Each of the five fingers consists of a group of individual building units with related pedestrian access. The buildings are four or five storeys high, containing apartments, each with two to four bedrooms and an open balcony. Each apartment is different in size, shape, layout and internal organisation, thus giving the individual family its own identity while, at the same time, by means of services and circulation, integrating it into the group.

Construction of the units was exclusively developed for this project and is based on prefabricated, industrialised and standardised concrete elements assembled on the site. It is the particular shape of these elements which makes the comprehensive housing scheme both functional and individual. They are designed on the form of the dodecahedron and the cube and the different ways they are able to interrelate. The geometry of the cube provides the inside lattice of the apartments' subdivision, while the dodecahedron envelops the outer shell of the building, forming the open balconies and integrating inside and outside of the structure.

*The rear elevation (above) looking onto the interior courtyard (the twelve-sided shapes contain bedrooms)*

*Five-sided structures enclosing balconies open to the sky (above, right)*

*The first phase of the housing project (right, middle)*

*View from the south-east towards the main pedestrian entrance (right, bottom)*

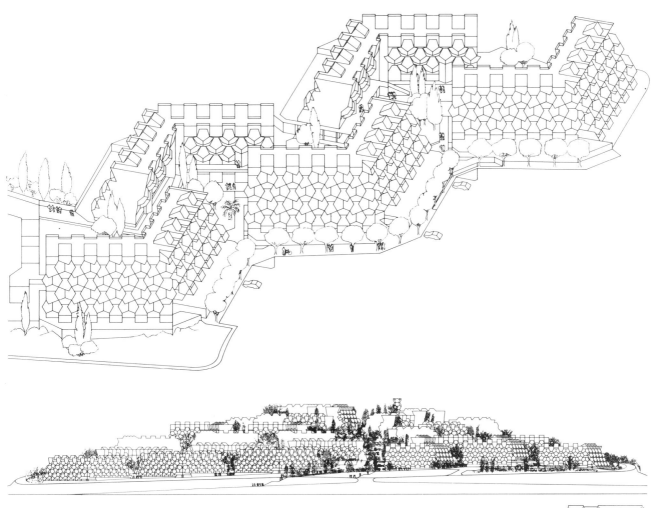

Iran

## DJAHANGUIR DARVICH AND RENÉ SARGER
### Stadium, Farahabad, Teheran
### (1977)

This large sports stadium in Teheran, designed by the French engineer René Sarger and Persian architect Djahanguir Darvich, is a marriage of modern western technology and local tradition. The stadium was commissioned by the Department for Sports Education. It was designed to accommodate 30,000 people and is part of a large *complex sportif* along French lines. Central attention is given to the roof system, which has a pre-stressed net structure that covers approximately 10,000 seats. The cable system is supported by two large masts, each 3 yds in diameter and 80 yds high. The result is a tensile structure on monumental dimensions which with a substructure of rein-forced concrete constitutes a large open sports area.

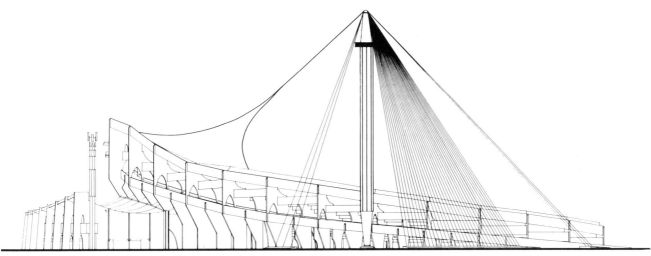

Entrance to the stadium (above, top)

South elevation (above)

Football field and athletics tracks (left, top)

Tensile roof structure (left)

India

## M. Y. THACKERAY AND CHARLES CORREA
### Vashi New Town, Bombay (1978)

The planning and building of new cities has been one of the most difficult tasks of architects in our time. The challenge has been particularly urgent in India, where housing for the fast-growing population has been neglected for decades. Under the chief architect and planner M. Y. Thackeray, with the cooperation of Charles Correa, the town of New Bombay is, internationally, one of the most promising solutions to date. In 1970 planning began for a new urban community of about two million inhabitants, which was partly completed by 1978. The new town includes several types of housing from low-rise apartment blocks to houses built in rows or grouped together. There are also shopping centres, social facilities, schools and kindergartens, and open spaces for community use. The new town is planned realistically in eight sectors.

*E-type apartment building in sector 1 (above, top)*

*A row of houses in sector 6 (above)*

*Side view of E-type apartment building in sector 1 (left)*

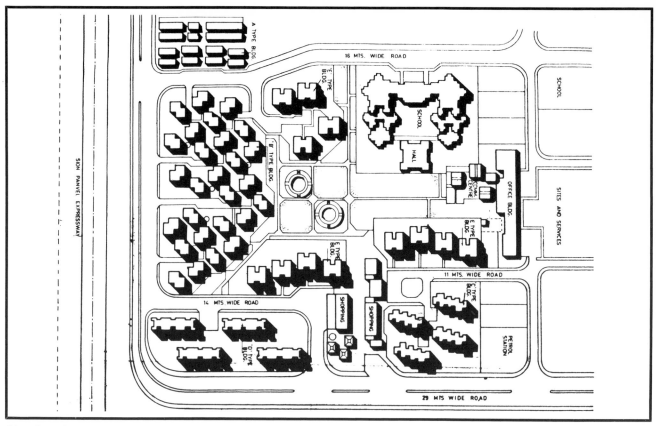

*Site plan of sector 1*

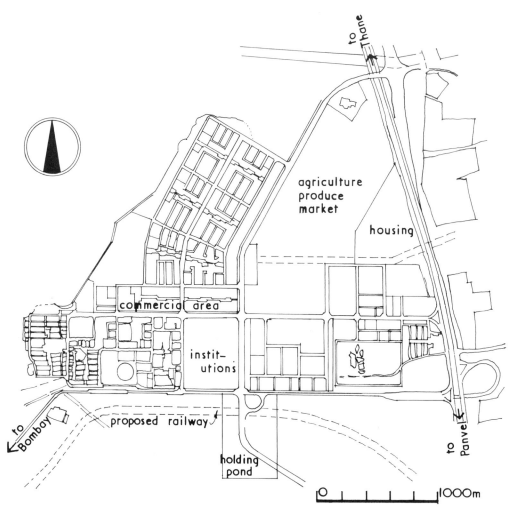

*Master plan showing land use*

122

# Thailand

## SUMET JUMSAI
### Science Museum, Bangkok
### (1977)

The Bangkok Science Museum is the first phase of a large complex in a park in Bangkok, and the first major work of an architectural firm in Thailand. The museum was built directly adjoining the existing planetarium, and forms a nucleus round which other buildings will eventually be erected. The surrounding trees and water ponds have been preserved as far as possible so they can be included in the final plan of this park.

The architects conceived of the museum as a modern technological building which gives the flexibility of space that its function demands. This was central to the design work from the beginning and the completed structure is an exciting articulation of the architects' concept.

The entrance is dominated from the outside by a large cantilevered roof, which leads into the main hall, where a view into the different areas of the museum is possible. The museum not only contains displays, but also has facilities for research, classrooms, a library, audio-visual departments, teachers' rooms, and a cafeteria.

The museum was designed as a transparent instrument for scientific display and public use, not as a closed research institute. To this end, even the inner research laboratories and administration areas are visually accessible.

*View inside main exhibit hall looking towards the central staircase*

123

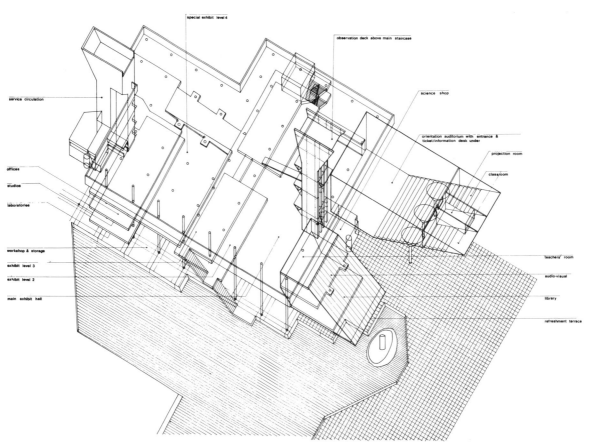

special exhibit level 4

observation deck above main staircase

service circulation

science shop

orientation auditorium with entrance & ticket/information desk under

projection room

class/room

offices

studios

laboratories

workshop & storage

exhibit level 3

exhibit level 2

main exhibit hall

teachers' room

audio-visual

library

refreshment terrace

*Axonometric (left)*

*Part of the north elevation (left, below)*

*View of the main entrance under the orientation auditorium (right)*

*North-west view at night (below)*

*Section (bottom)*

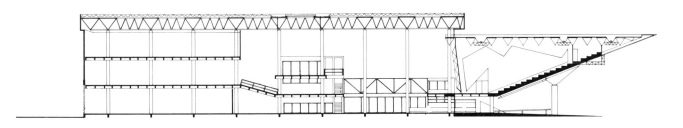

125

Singapore

## WILLIAM S. W. LIM AND DESIGN PARTNERSHIP
### Golden Mile Shopping Centre, Singapore
### (1969–72)

In 1964 the government of Singapore began an urban renewal programme to replace an old area of squatters and marine industries. The Golden Mile Shopping Centre, located between Nicoll Highway and Beach Road at one end of the Golden Mile in Singapore, was the first building completed in this programme. The large complex includes shops in the three lower floors, offices above, and luxury flats on the higher levels with a view of the seafront. This has created a building catering for a variety of uses, and helping in the revitalisation of that part of the city. There are plans to add a hotel and other office facilities. Commercial architecture on a large scale by local developers is of great significance in South East Asia.

*Interior detail (above)*

*Ground floor plan*

*View from the street (right)*

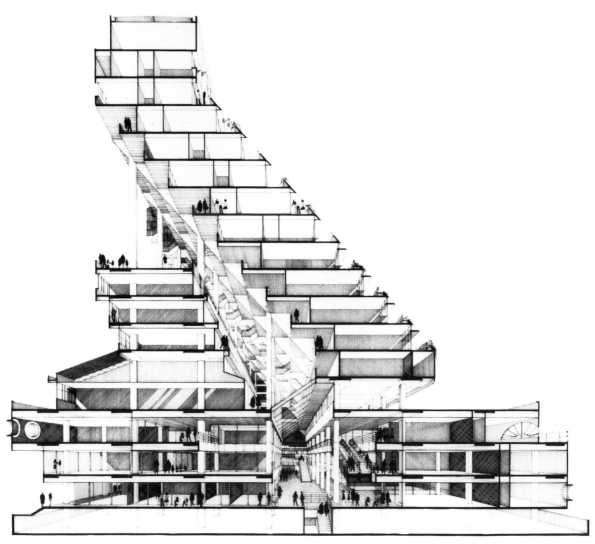

Sectional perspective

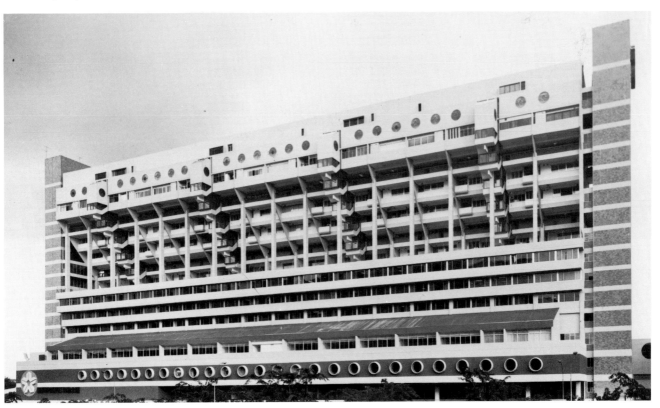

Main façade

127

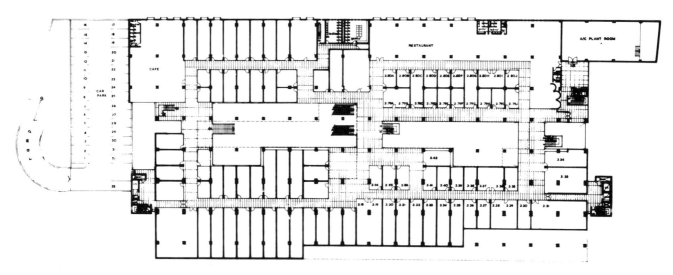

**Australia**

## JOHN ANDREWS
### Cameron Offices, Canberra
### (1969–77)

Andrews's Cameron offices have to be seen as part of the future urban fabric of Belconnen, one of the few new towns around Canberra. The building is located on the ridge of a small hill on Black Mountain, about 11 miles from the centre of Canberra. Commissioned by the National Capital Development Commission it is designed to house 4000 civil servants. The client first visualised the offices as a vertical tower, but the architect's plan emerged as a large megastructural environment with the office wings linked to the main spine or public street. These wings are separated by gardens on a linear plan. The main street of the complex links the office wings which run perpendicular to it. On it are shops, a supermarket, liquor store and a newsagent; it thus combines government offices with commercial facilities. South of the building is a plan for housing which, when it is built, will incorporate the administration into the new community.

*Restaurant area*

129

*Model of the complete scheme (above)*

*View from the lake (left, above)*

*General view at night (left)*

# Hong Kong

## TAO HO
## Hong Kong Arts Centre, Hong Kong
## (1974–77)

The Hong Kong Arts Centre, located on the waterfront, is a cultural focal point, where the visual and performing arts are united under one roof. Its 19 storeys, two of them underground, contain two theatres—one with 463 seats, the other with 100 seats—exhibition spaces, artists' studios, a recital hall with 200 seats, a restaurant, club rooms, office space, and a sculpture garden. The tower, used as the main design motif, repeating itself in the structural grid, is triangular, which maximises the existing space. Structural elements are used as part of the decorative pattern as in old Chinese architecture. The material of the building is based on reinforced concrete.

*Front elevation*

*Hanging air-conditioned duct in the entrance lobby (above right)*

*Floor plans of the recital hall and exhibition galleries (below right)*

1—Recital hall, 2—Void over studio theatre, 3—Foyer, 4—Projection room, 5—Storage, 6—Void over rehearsal room, 7—Exhibition gallery, 8—Sculpture gallery, 9—Void over stage (scenery flytower), 10—Air conditioning room

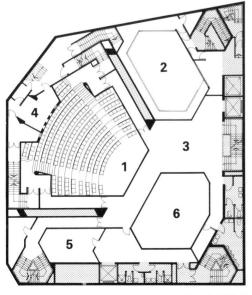

**Recital Hall**

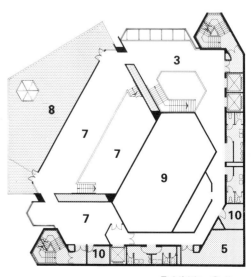

**Exhibition Gallery**

*Third floor lobby leading to the balcony of the main theatre*

1—Circulation/services/structural zone, 2—
M + E structural zone, 3—Ceiling structural grid,

4—Chimney, 5—Air conditioning
room, 6—Storage, 7—Light well

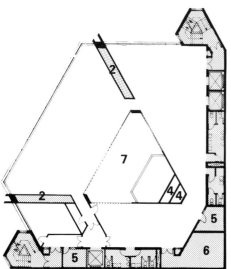 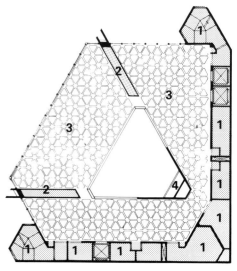

*Typical floor plan (left) and structural grid and service cores (right)*

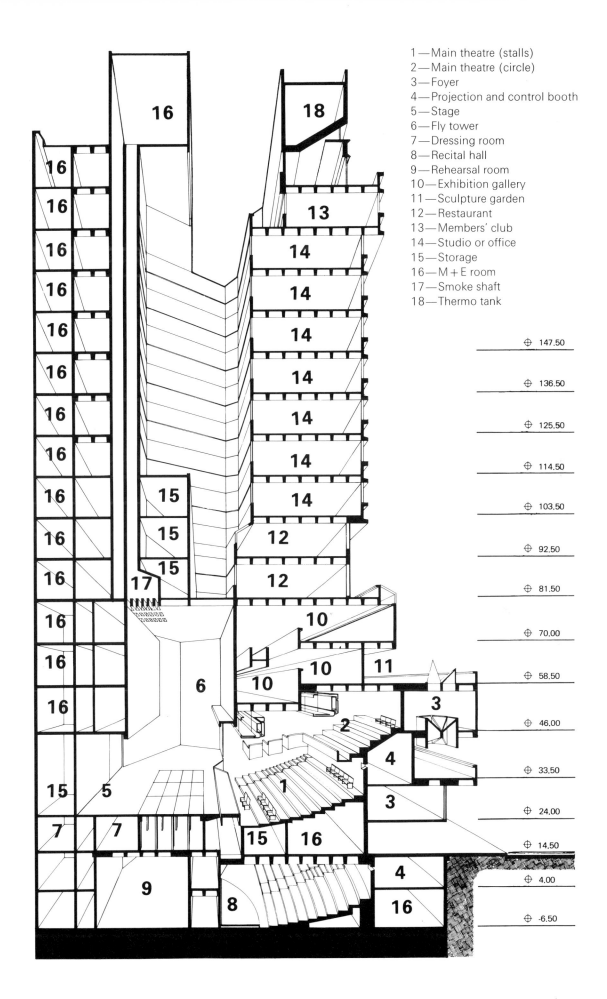

1—Main theatre (stalls)
2—Main theatre (circle)
3—Foyer
4—Projection and control booth
5—Stage
6—Fly tower
7—Dressing room
8—Recital hall
9—Rehearsal room
10—Exhibition gallery
11—Sculpture garden
12—Restaurant
13—Members' club
14—Studio or office
15—Storage
16—M + E room
17—Smoke shaft
18—Thermo tank

⊕ 147.50

⊕ 136.50

⊕ 125.50

⊕ 114.50

⊕ 103.50

⊕ 92.50

⊕ 81.50

⊕ 70.00

⊕ 58.50

⊕ 46.00

⊕ 33.50

⊕ 24.00

⊕ 14.50

⊕ 4.00

⊕ -6.50

*Section*

135

# Japan

## KISHO KUROKAWA
### City Hall, Waki
### (1975)

Public buildings today are conceived more and more in the spirit of public participation and are no longer seen as the symbol of power of the city administration. Kurokawa's city hall in Waki is one of the best examples of this change of direction. The building consists of an administrative block on one side, and council rooms on the other, joined by bridge corridors on the third floor. Most important is the space separating them, which is a public plaza. In Kurokawa's own terms this is not defined as a garden, but as the 'en-space', the space in-between.

From outside, the complex appears as a rectangular block, but on entering it, one immediately finds oneself in the plaza, which leads to both the administration wing and the council chambers. The open space is not merely in-between the two wings, it is the connecting element.

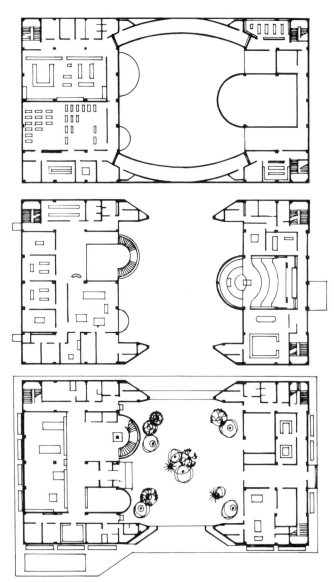

*Approach to the city hall (right)*

*The hall in its town setting (below right)*

*Floor plans: second floor (top), first floor (middle) and ground floor (bottom)*

Fish-eye view of the interior

*The council chamber*

*Cross-section*

# FUMIHIKO MAKI
## National Aquarium, Okinawa
## (1974–75)

The theme of the 1975 International Exposition in Okinawa was 'the sea we would like to see'. Many of the pavilions were dedicated to the study of ichthyology. Maki designed and built the only permanent structure in the exhibition, the National Aquarium. This exemplary building is a landmark in the design of aquariums.

The site is bound on the east by a cliff, and on the west by an irregular coastline. The building consists of an aquarium proper, a dolphin island, a plaza, and a green area. The fish tanks contain fish from all over the world.

In recognition of the hot subtropical climate, strong protection against the sun was necessary. Maki devised a scheme of prefabricated arcades around the periphery of the aquarium. The prefabricated elements were poured adjacent to the site. This system of semi-circular arcades is the identifying feature of this attractive building.

*The main entrance (right)*

*Ground floor plan showing line of sections (right, below)*

*Part of the system of arcades around the building (below)*

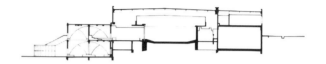

*Section A—A*

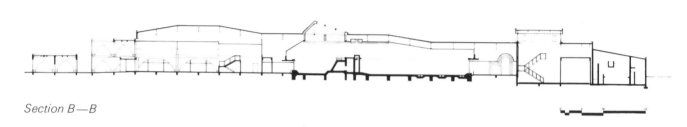

*Section B—B*

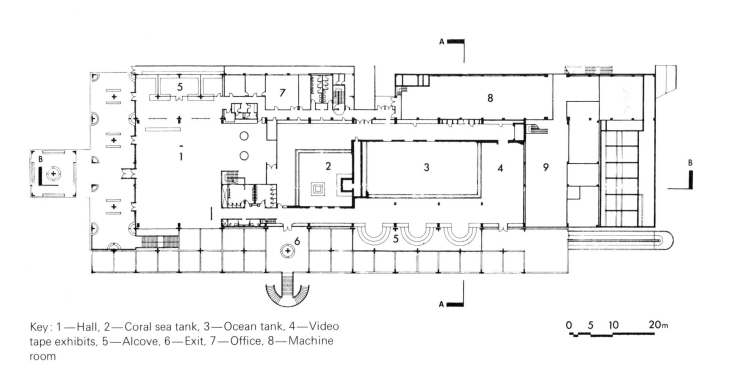

Key: 1—Hall, 2—Coral sea tank, 3—Ocean tank, 4—Video tape exhibits, 5—Alcove, 6—Exit, 7—Office, 8—Machine room

0  5  10    20m

# KIYONORI KIKUTAKE
## Aquapolis, Okinawa
## (1975)

Japanese architects have developed the relationship between architecture and technology further than architects elsewhere. Kikutake's Aquapolis is the culmination of his earlier experiments with platforms above the ocean and is also one of the first realistic manifestations of this type of architecture. Built for the 1975 exhibition in Okinawa in collaboration with the Mitsubishi Heavy Industries, it resembles an off-shore oil rig. It is based on eight vertical round cores set into and fixed to the ocean floor. A square platform above provides an artificial floor. This island has an exhibition hall, a conference room and its own power generators, sewage disposal system and seawater conversion apparatus. It is thus, to a large extent, independent of the resources of the mainland. The platform stands 60 ft above the water, and occupies an area of 2·5 acres. It can be seen as a model of how technology can serve architectural visions in the exploration of new territories.

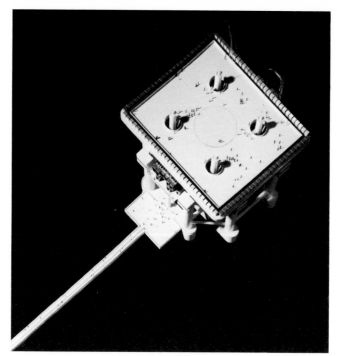

*Aerial view of model*

*Side view of the Aquapolis*

142

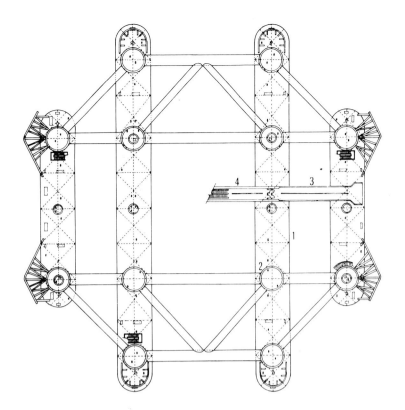

*Lower hull plan*

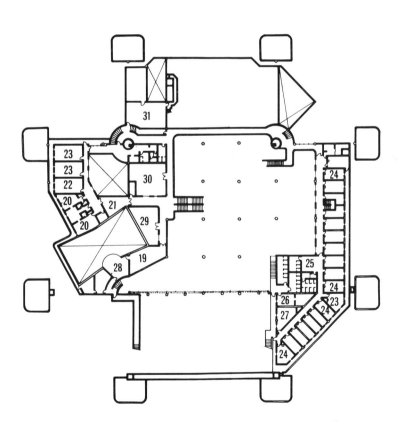

*Middle deck plan*

| | | | |
|---|---|---|---|
| 1—Lower hull | 10—Seagull bridge | 19—Office | 28—Machine room |
| 2—Column | 11—Aquapolis model | 20—VIP room | 29—Control room |
| 3—Pedestrian deck | 12—Information booth | 21—VIP lobby | 30—Computer room |
| 4—Escalator tube | 13—Aqua farming | 22—Governmental room | 31—Utility control room |
| 5—Aqua hall | 14—Machine space | 23—Executive room | 32—Heliport |
| 6—Marinorama | 15—Dining room | 24—Staff room | 33—Monument |
| 7—Marinorama | 16—Pantry | 25—Staff lobby | 34—Chimney |
| 8—Marine forest | 17—Office | 26—Companion room | 35—Artificial lawn |
| 9—Moving belt | 18—Aqua port | 27—Recreation room | 36—Tent |

143

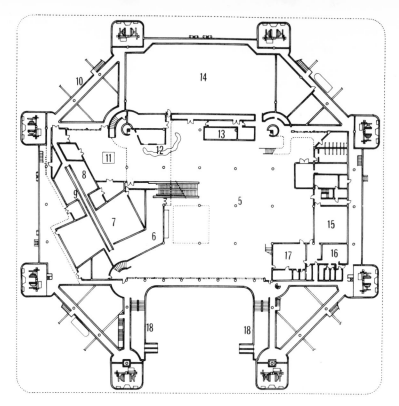

*Main deck plan*

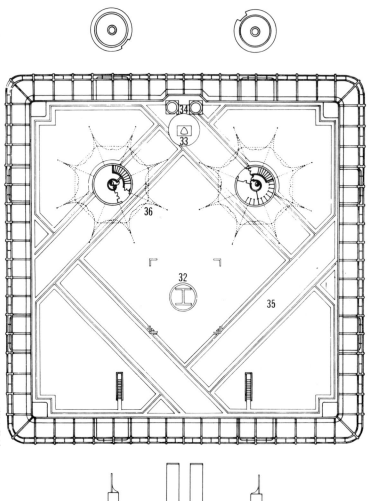

*Upper deck plan*

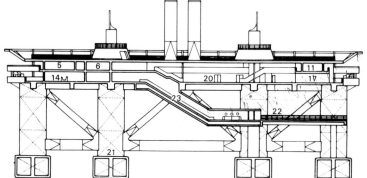

144    *Section*

# TAKAMITSU AZUMA
## Seijin Nursery School, Kyoto
## (1973–74)

A large number of buildings in the seventies were devoted to tasks of social care for children and people with special needs. Azuma's Nursery School is one of these structures where a new concept has been articulated for these requirements. Two main blocks, surrounding a courtyard, contain a playroom and auditorium on the ground floor and nursing space on the first.

The architect aimed at creating space in which there was a flexibility that allowed the children to play and mingle as freely as possible, within the safety requirements. Architecturally this is visible in the balconies, large courtyard and covered galleries, all on a scale which relates to the children. To fulfill its particular requirements, this building creates a closed-in environment, isolating its activities as far as possible from the urban space surrounding it.

*The central courtyard (right)*

*Main entrance (below)*

*Children playing in the central courtyard*

146

*Play areas*

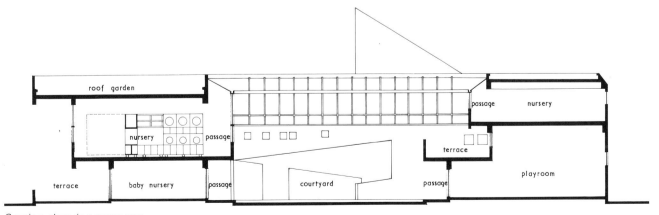

*Section showing room use*

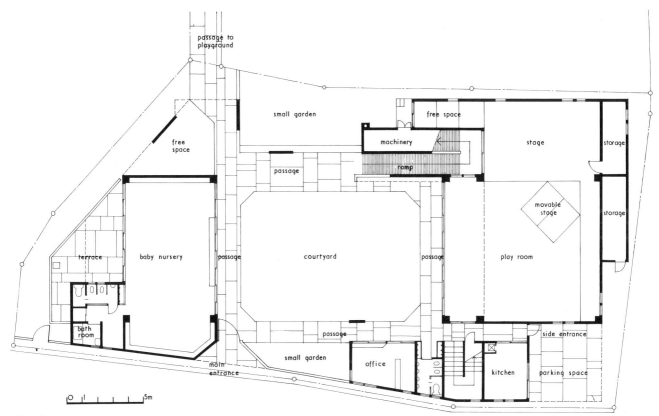

passage to
playground

small garden

free
space

free space

machinery

ramp

stage

storage

movable
stage

terrace          baby nursery          passage          courtyard          passage          play room          storage

bath
room

passage          passage

main
entrance          small garden          office          kitchen          side entrance

parking space

0    1                    5m

*First floor plan*

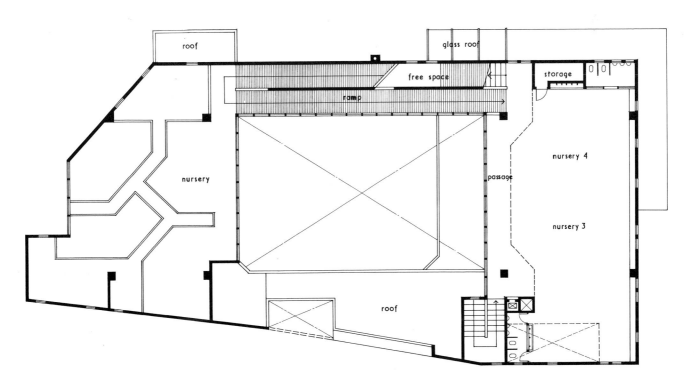

roof

glass roof

free space

storage

ramp

nursery          nursery 4          passage          nursery 3

roof

*Ground floor plan*